AF304740

# CONTENTS

# 1.
# Origins:
# Bradford, 1937–59

London seemed as far away as America when David Hockney was growing up. On the street where his family lived, nobody had ever been. He was eighteen when he first went to the capital – before then, his world was centred on the market town of Bradford, the home of Britain's wool trade. He was born there in 1937, the fourth of five children, into a family whose home was typical of their working-class Yorkshire community – a two-bedroom terraced house at the top of a steep hill, with an outdoor toilet and a coal hole for a garden. His sister, Margaret, two years older than him, remembered the house on Steadman Terrace as a place of darkness.

Hockney's parents had met through the local Methodist Mission – Laura was a Sunday school teacher, as well as working in a draper's shop – and they had married in 1929. Kenneth was an accounts clerk in a local firm of drysalters, and a man of culture and principle. In the 1920s, he had attended evening classes at the art school in Bradford, on topics such as 'light and shade'. Haunted by the memory of his brother returning from the First World War, ravaged by poison gas, Kenneth registered as a conscientious objector during the Second World War. He was forced to wash away the word 'Coward', daubed on the wall by a neighbour, before going to work.

During the bombing raids of the early 1940s, the family used to take shelter in a cupboard under the stairs. One of Hockney's earliest memories is the sound of his mother's scream as a bomb dropped on their street. In 1943, they moved to a terraced Victorian house in Eccleshill, a suburb in the north of Bradford known for its nineteenth-century mills, where he shared an attic bedroom with his younger brother. To the children's delight, Kenneth renovated the interior of the home by veneering the panelled doors in sheets of hardboard and painting a sunset onto each. Hockney took a thrill, also, in watching his father refurbish old bicycles, painting them in new colours and adorning the bars with wonderfully straight lines brushed in freehand.

An ardent pacifist and atheist, Kenneth frequently wrote letters to world leaders including the pope and Mahatma Gandhi. In later years, Hockney liked to tell the story of how his father heaved an armchair down to the local phone box (the Hockneys didn't have a landline) and sat there reading, having placed an advertisement in the local newspaper asking interested clients to call the phone box at a certain time on Sunday morning. 'Never worry about what the neighbours think' was Kenneth's advice to his children – an attitude more aristocratic, perhaps, than working class. But the young Hockney took it to heart.

Kenneth lost his job soon after VE Day, possibly due to his pacifist beliefs. The family never had much money. When Hockney won a scholarship to Bradford Grammar

School in 1948, at the age of eleven, he had to wear a secondhand blazer. For the majority of his time at school, he was 'terribly bored', although he found transient relief in designing posters for school events and submitting drawings to the school magazine. He deliberately underperformed in academic subjects so as not to have to drop art. An English teacher made the sardonic remark: 'he still does not believe that an artist occasionally needs to use words.' In maths lessons, he made surreptitious drawings of the little cacti that the master had lined up on the windowsill. When, at the age of eleven, he told the headmaster that he intended to become an artist, he was counselled that there would be time later for such an ambition.

Aged twelve, Hockney came across lines by the seventeenth-century poet George Herbert that would later resonate with his interest in mirrors and pools. The words – part of a hymn sung at school – evoke both containment and transcendental aspiration:

> A man that looks on glass,
> On it may stay his eye;
> Or if he pleaseth, through it pass,
> And then the heav'n espy.

In his early teens, he worked for two summers on a farm near the village of Huggate, sixty miles to the east of Bradford. Cycling around the low hills of the Yorkshire Wolds, he became intimately acquainted with the landscape that would become a dominant subject of his work half a century later. He remembered being very happy working in the fields, stooking (or sheaving) corn. It was a monotonous job, but for the first time Hockney was away from home unsupervised. He and the other labourers slept in four large double beds in one room. 'It was all very male,' he recalled.

His father subsisted on a modest income: for a time, building dolls' prams and reconditioning real prams served as his main source of money. And yet Hockney was able, as a child and a teenager, to visit the cinema ('the pictures') regularly – the family didn't own a television until he was eighteen. He would travel there on the top deck of a bus, seated at the front so that he could see more from the windows. The films that he watched in these years would have a lasting impact – he has often said that he was brought up in Hollywood and Bradford ('Hollywood was at the end of the street, in the local cinema'). A snapshot of Hockney at the age of sixteen shows him in Chaplinesque guise, wearing a bowler hat and suit and holding a walking stick. His father was a fan of Laurel and Hardy. When Hockney saw *Big Business* (1929), in which the duo played Christmas tree salesmen, he noticed the strong shadows that were cast on the roads in the Californian summer.

Kenneth took the children to concerts, too – as many as three a week during the music season. At the age of ten, Hockney saw a production – at the Alhambra Theatre – of Puccini's *La Bohème*. Bradford had more in the way of music, he later stated, than visual art, and his musical education consisted entirely of live events. The local art gallery contained mostly Victorian paintings, and while Leeds had a broader variety, including a few Rembrandts, there was nothing in the way of modern art.

Hockney's parents were sceptical at first about his wish to transfer to art school. They thought he should get a job, perhaps as a commercial artist. When someone told him that he would require further training for this, he happily relayed the advice to his mother. Before long, his parents were persuaded. He left the grammar school for Bradford College of Art in September 1953, at the age of sixteen, having obtained a scholarship of £40 a year to study painting. This was a liberation from the tedium and restriction of life at school, although the curriculum and culture of the art college were traditional, with a strong focus on drawing from observation.

'When I went to art school,' Hockney later reminisced, 'a neighbour said, "Some of the people in the art school just don't work at all. Lazy buggers." And I said, "Oh I am going to work, don't worry." And I did.' He worked all day on exercises in perspective, anatomy and other foundations of an artist's training, taking particular pleasure in drawing from life models. Sometimes he stayed on for the evening classes that were intended for amateurs.

This period marked the beginning of Hockney's prolific output. He painted domestic scenes, people at leisure and the urban landscape. In 1954, he was enthralled by an exhibition at the Edinburgh Festival about the career of Sergei Diaghilev, the Russian ballet impresario – and in particular by Diaghilev's embrace of his sexuality. It was at this time, too, that he encountered the first professional artist he had ever met. Jacob Kramer was a Ukrainian-born painter whose family had settled in Leeds in 1900, escaping the persecution of Jews in the Russian empire. Kramer had studied at the Slade in 1913–14, before returning to Leeds where he became a local celebrity. Hockney saw his paintings in the city gallery and was impressed by the fact that Kramer lived from his work, without teaching.

When not in the art school, Hockney would walk around the town, often dressed in a bowler hat and moleskin trousers, pushing a pram that contained his painting materials. He would paint the streets of Eccleshill on used canvases picked up from junk shops. In those days, he remarked later, he was always trying to avoid L.S. Lowry a bit. The resulting scenes of terraced houses or more well-to-do detached residences carried echoes of the Euston Road School of the late 1930s and 1940s, exuding a stark 'kitchen sink' realism. The influence of Walter Sickert remained pervasive.

A 1957 portrait of the artist's father, showing Kenneth seated and introspective in a jacket and tie and waistcoat, was the first work that Hockney sold: he sent the painting to an exhibition of Yorkshire artists in Leeds, where it made £10. During the creation of the work, Hockney's father had set up a sequence of mirrors (one of them appears in the background of the picture) so that he could review progress. He would offer advice as his son worked: 'that's too muddy, is that for my cheek? No, no, it's not that colour.'

At the age of eighteen, Hockney hitchhiked to London and saw a variety of modern paintings for the first time. He became increasingly eager, during his four years at the art college in Bradford, for new artistic knowledge and experiences. He knew that London was where he needed to be in order to develop. Bradford was rigidly academic and impervious to modern art – he even came to wonder whether his time there had afforded him anything of use. And so he sent folders of his work to the Slade School of Art and the Royal College of Art (RCA), and was invited for interview at both. On his way to the Slade interview, he lost a tooth. The mishap didn't prevent his being offered a place, and yet it was to the RCA – more avant-garde in spirit – that he decided to head, accepting an offer to start there in September 1959.

First, though, he had to suffer the ordeal of national service. Unwilling to join the colonial war that was being fought in Cyprus, Hockney registered as a conscientious objector. He worked in St Luke's Hospital, Bradford, as an orderly on the skin diseases ward. He hated the job, although he did occasionally take the opportunity to sketch patients. During these two years, he also designed posters for the Campaign for Nuclear Disarmament and became a vegetarian, like his mother (although he never adopted her teetotalism or his parents' shared antipathy for smoking: a fragment of old footage shot in Bradford shows Kenneth Hockney trying in exasperation to grab a cigarette out of his son's mouth). A more pleasant phase was spent in Hastings in 1958–59, staying in a cottage with a group of friends. Around this time, Hockney began to experiment for the first time with abstraction.

# 2.
# Adhesiveness: London and New York, 1960–63

The only rule at the RCA was that life drawing was compulsory. Other than that, it was the ideal setting for a free spirit such as Hockney. Students were largely left to their own devices. The three years that he spent there were more than simply formative: they represented the birth of his artistic persona.

His circle of friends quickly came to include Allen Jones, Patrick Caulfield, Adrian Berg and Ron ('R.B.') Kitaj. These men, Hockney realised, were the core of the more experimental faction of students – engaged in the art of their own time, not mired in the methods and principles of a bygone era. Large-scale abstract painting was the in-vogue style. Abstract Expressionism had been the subject of a major show at the Tate Gallery in 1959. Hockney had also seen the 1958 exhibition of Jackson Pollock's paintings at the Whitechapel Art Gallery; he considered these heroic, the first modern paintings not to be influenced by Picasso. He undertook some large-scale AbEx experiments but found the results 'barren'. It was the American-born Kitaj, an advocate of figurative art, who advised him: 'Painting is research. Your work should explore what most interests you.'

Kitaj, who arrived at the RCA on the same day as Hockney, was four years older. Born in Ohio of European parents and impressively worldly, he had travelled extensively as a sailor and had lived in Vienna. Hockney had still never been abroad. Yet their admiration was mutual. In their first week, Kitaj witnessed Hockney drawing a skeleton in the cast gallery. He considered it the most beautiful drawing he had ever seen in an art school and paid £5 for it. In the second week, Hockney made a more elaborate skeleton drawing. Kitaj acquired this, too – but many years later, via a dealer, and for considerably more money.

The skeleton drawings were the culmination of Hockney's academic training, both an ending and a starting point. Kitaj's friendship and counsel helped meanwhile to alleviate Hockney's insecurity about being a provincial Yorkshire boy. He became inured to other students' mockery of his accent ('Trouble at t'mill, Mr Ormondroyd'). Adhering to Kitaj's advice to explore 'what most interests you', he began to combine abstract (or semi-abstract) imagery with words, whether fragments of poetry or graffiti remembered from toilet walls. Words offered a way of crystallising the feeling inherent in a painting.

Through this pairing of elements, Hockney gave voice to his own burgeoning sense of self, above all his sexuality. A painting titled *Yellow Abstract* from 1960, made in oil and sand on canvas, included the barely legible word 'Queer'. *Doll Boy* (1960–61) came soon after, a picture of a man wearing a dress inscribed with the word 'Queen'. *Adhesiveness* (1960), made at the start of his second year at the RCA, was more explicit. Two diagrammatic men are seen locked in a '69' position. Numerical labels identify the participants in the scene (numbers standing for initials – a trick Hockney had learned from the American poet Walt Whitman, whose boldly homoerotic verse he was reading voraciously): Hockney (4.8), Whitman (23.23) and, in smaller letters, suggesting an afterthought, Cliff Richard (3.18), who was Hockney's pin-up in those days. The deliberately childish works of Jean Dubuffet were a dominant influence, but so too were literary sources such as the works of Whitman and Constantine Cavafy, introduced to him by Adrian Berg.

Berg was one of the first openly gay people Hockney met. Another was Quentin Crisp, who modelled regularly at the RCA. Hockney later remembered how Crisp used to go around the drawings and make comments – sometimes telling Hockney that his efforts weren't any good. Crisp, who spent thirty years as a life model in London's art schools, would later make his film debut in the RCA's low-budget production of *Hamlet* (1976); he became a queer icon and national figure (one of the 'stately homos of England', in his own saying) following the film adaptation of his autobiography, *The Naked Civil Servant*, in 1975. Figures such as Berg and Crisp, unabashed about their sexuality, provided Hockney with the impetus to live the same way. The RCA was part of bohemia in those days, and he has frequently observed that this tolerant, liberated world made it possible for him to be open.

Hockney came to regard *Adhesiveness*, with its interlocking bodies and layered references, as his first really serious painting. The photographer Cecil Beaton, then at the height of his celebrity as a chronicler of high society, bought the work for £40 on one of his visits to the college. It was around this time, too, that Hockney discovered printing and learned how to etch – a fortuitous development, given that he couldn't always afford painting materials. Even so, he felt himself to be rich by student standards. He was already selling his paintings, and he could afford to buy packets of twenty cigarettes instead of the standard ten.

In his early days at the RCA, Hockney spent much of his time in the little cubicle he had been allocated to paint in, regarding it almost as his home. On one occasion, he was discovered by Carel Weight, the professor of painting, bathing in the sink. His actual home was hardly less makeshift – a shed at the bottom of a garden in Earl's Court, with a single bed and an electric heater.

In the spring of 1960, at the Marlborough gallery in Mayfair, Hockney encountered the work of Francis Bacon. He was struck by Bacon's distorted nudes, later remarking: 'One of the things I liked about them was that you could smell the balls.' The influence of Bacon's bleary physiognomies can be traced in the central bent head of *Doll Boy*. In July, Hockney went to the giant Picasso exhibition at the Tate Gallery – the first blockbuster show of its kind, and the moment when Picasso and European Modernism decisively arrived in Britain. The show precipitated a wave of what the newspapers called Picassomania. Hockney was spellbound. The freedom and experimentation that he discerned in the works of the Spanish master would inspire him throughout his life. He returned to the Picasso show seven times that summer.

Early the following year, a young art dealer, John Kasmin, visited the Young Contemporaries exhibition at the RBA Galleries on Suffolk Street, in which Hockney and several RCA contemporaries were included. The arrangement of their works in a defined grouping signalled the arrival of Pop Art, although most of them shunned the term. Kasmin bought *Doll Boy* for £40, intrigued by its combination of abstraction and figuration. He later recollected the profound, seductive impact of the young artist:

> When I met him at the show, I found him shy, sweet, trusting and nice in his black crewcut hair and glasses. He had a sort of gifted impudence which really attracted me. And he obviously had an extraordinary natural talent. I knew he would be a success, and his open homosexuality and use of gay imagery would be to his advantage since gay people always have money to spend on art.

Kasmin had started out as a poet, before cutting his teeth as an art dealer in the late 1950s at Victor Musgrave's Gallery One in Soho, where, for a time, he slept on a board over the bathtub. By the time he visited the Young Contemporaries show of 1961, he was in his mid-twenties and working at the more upmarket Marlborough. He tried to interest his bosses in Hockney's work. But the gallery's co-founder, Harry Fischer, considered it scruffy: he would only allow Kasmin to keep a few paintings behind a curtain, out of public view. Kasmin left Marlborough shortly after and became Hockney's dealer and agent, with the support of

Sheridan Hamilton-Temple-Blackwood, the Marquess of Dufferin and Ava, an aspiring patron of the arts. Kas, as he became known, first showed Hockney's work in his Earl's Court flat, selling paintings for £50 to £100.

The blessing of saleability would never desert him – from this time on, Hockney lived by his art. In July 1961, at the start of the summer vacation, he embarked on a two-month trip to the USA, having discovered $99 fares on the charter airline Flying Tiger. He paid for the trip using prize money from the John Moores exhibition in Liverpool, a Guinness Award for etching, and a commission (awarded to several RCA students) to redecorate the SS *Canberra*, an ocean liner. He loved New York. He felt at once that it was the place to be, a city that ran twenty-four hours a day. Soon after arriving, he headed for the Museum of Modern Art, carrying a letter of introduction from a London tutor to the curator William S. Lieberman. To his profound surprise, Hockney managed to sell Lieberman a cache of etchings.

This sale later became the subject of *Receiving an Inheritance*, one of a sequence of etchings based on Hockney's adventures in New York and modelled on William Hogarth's 1730s 'modern moral' series *A Rake's Progress*. Hockney began work on his own *Rake's Progress* series upon his return to London in September 1961 and completed it in 1963, after a subsequent visit to New York. One source of inspiration for the series was the spectacle of homelessness and squalor in the Bowery – for Hockney, this conjured visions of eighteenth-century London.

On Long Beach, close to New York, he stayed with Mark Berger, a friend from the RCA. Berger had first come to

Hockney's attention when he plastered the walls of his cubicle with pages from gay magazines. A photograph from the trip shows Hockney, his hair dark and cropped, smoking a cigar on the beach. A drawing titled *Mark Berger, Long Beach* shows Berger with the logo of Camel cigarettes balanced on his head, a motif that Hockney may have picked up from the American painter Larry Rivers.

American brands loomed large. One evening, as Hockney and Berger watched television with friends, an advertisement for Lady Clairol hair dye flashed up on the television: 'Blondes have more fun. Doors open for a blonde.' Hockney declared on the spot that he would dye his hair, and persuaded Berger and the others to do the same. An early plate of *A Rake's Progress* shows Hockney's naked upper body beneath a bottle of Lady Clairol, as he gazes through an open door. Below the image, a legend reads: 'The start of the spending spree and the door opening for a blonde.'

Hockney stayed blond from that point. His mother assumed that his hair had been bleached by the sun, and she became so used to his appearance that she would subsequently claim that he had been born blond. From Long Beach, the newly peroxided Hockney decamped to Brooklyn to stay with Ferrill Amacker, a painter and photographer whom he had met through Berger. In Amacker's company he toured New York's gay scene, an adventure reflected in the darker, wilder phase of the *Rake's Progress* etchings.

Hockney spent the remainder of his trip in Amacker's well-heeled apartment, where their friendship was sexual from time to time, although Hockney's record of the experience is elliptical: 'I met a boy in a drugstore in Times Square and stayed with him for three months.' The galleries and museums of New York were also a draw. Towards the end of his trip, he met Claes Oldenburg – the only established American artist he encountered – while Oldenburg was installing papier-mâché sculptures of shirts and ties for a group show at the Green Gallery in midtown Manhattan.

When Hockney returned to the RCA in late 1961, the registrar, Mr Moon, recorded a wry note about his changed appearance: 'He visited the United States in the summer, and returned with a yellow crewcut, smoking cigars and wearing white shoes. I think it was the funniest sight I have ever seen! However, that is wearing off; the cigars have all run out, and I imagine he has pawned his shoes.' Despite Mr Moon's prediction of a toning-down, Hockney became more flamboyant in his appearance. He commonly wore odd socks, and he cut a provocative figure at the college's 1961 Christmas show, where he wore a blond wig, silk skirt and busty sequinned top, and sang 'I'm Just a Girl Who Can't Say No'.

Hockney had been persuaded to perform his drag act by Ferrill Amacker, who was passing through London on his way to Italy to stay with Mark Berger. Amacker talked Hockney into accompanying him to Europe rather than returning to Bradford for Christmas. A teacher at the college offered them a lift in his van as far as Switzerland, provided they share the price of the petrol. For Hockney, who agreed to sit in the back of the vehicle, the journey was uncomfortable and eventless. He saw hardly any of the Gothic landscapes he had eagerly anticipated. In the painting *Flight into Italy – Swiss Landscape* (1962), he depicted the experience. The mountains are based on a diagram from a geography book, except for a tiny realistic fragment (taken from a postcard) of a snow-clad peak. Hockney is shown cramped in the back of a hurtling van, while words spew from the rear of the vehicle: 'thats Switzerland that was'.

For the Young Contemporaries exhibition of February 1962, Hockney presented four paintings of dramatically different styles, albeit with the same subtitle – 'Demonstration of Versatility' – an explicit statement of his desire to multiply his range. This desire found expression, too, in his self-presentation. In July, at the RCA's convocation ceremony, he was awarded the gold medal for work of outstanding distinction and went to collect the award wearing a gold lamé jacket in place of an academic gown. The jacket made another appearance the following May, when Lord Snowdon, husband of Princess Margaret, photographed him in front of his painting *Domestic Scene, Los Angeles*, and going shopping with a matching gold bag, for *The Sunday Times*.

In the summer of 1962, Hockney travelled with the young American Jeff Goodman – a new love interest whom he had met by chance in the Arts Council Shop on Baker Street – to Florence, to visit Berger and Amacker. From Italy, they went on to Rome and Berlin. Hockney had been drawn to the latter city by the novels of Christopher Isherwood, although he was disappointed to find little in the way of Weimar decadence, except for the gay-friendly Kleist Casino with its pink lampshades.

Back in London that autumn, he chanced upon a friend in the street, who tipped him off about a flat to rent at 17 Powis Terrace, Notting Hill, then a rundown quarter of west London. Hockney visited and fell in love with the flat. The rent was five pounds a week. Kasmin agreed to put up the deposit in exchange for storage space, and so Hockney obtained the lease. He turned the largest room into his studio, sleeping on a small bed in the corner, at the end of which he positioned a sign: 'GET UP AND WORK IMMEDIATELY.'

The Powis Terrace flat became the tea-drinking epicentre of Hockney's social circle, despite its perpetual state of disarray. The artist Patrick Procktor would come over from Kentish Town to play chess late into the evening. The painting *Domestic Scene, Notting Hill Gate* (1963) shows Hockney's friend Mo McDermott standing naked on the artist's bed amid a sparse interior, and – seated in a chintz-covered armchair – Ossie Clark, a young fashion designer on the brink of stardom. Hockney had met Ossie and his girlfriend, Celia Birtwell, a textiles designer, through Mo. Ossie and Celia, along with Hockney himself, would shortly come to epitomise the Swinging London of the mid-1960s.

A complementary work, *Domestic Scene, Los Angeles* (1963), shows two youths – one naked, the other almost naked apart from sports socks and a napkin-like loincloth – in a sparse, flattened space. The first stands beneath a running shower, caught in a beam of blue colour that mimics the flow of the water, while the second reaches out to touch his shoulder. The work was made entirely from imagination. Hockney would not visit California until 1964. But it can be read as a prophetic statement, as well as a bold expression of desire. The poses of the two figures were derived from *Physique Pictorial*, a gay erotic magazine of the kind he had already used in *Life Painting for Diploma* (1962), his final assignment at the RCA.

John Kasmin opened his own gallery in New Bond Street in March 1963, with an exhibition of target paintings by Kenneth Noland. The gallery was unlike anything the London art world had seen – a high, white-walled room with a rubber floor, accessed via a narrow passageway that gave no forewarning of the spacious Modernist temple beyond. That December, Kasmin gave Hockney a solo show. Hockney was something of the odd man out in Kasmin's stable of American and British abstract painters, which included Jules Olitski, Dick Smith and Robyn Denny. As if to reinforce the point, the title of his show was *Paintings with People In*. But the show was a critical and commercial triumph. Almost every work sold, and the critic John Russell proclaimed in *The Sunday Times* that Hockney 'has given foreign visitors something to bite on when they ask what is happening in British art'.

Not long before, the rights to Hockney's series *A Rake's Progress* had been sold to the publisher Paul Cornwall-Jones, of Alecto Editions, for £5,000. Following this windfall and the success of the Kasmin show, he realised that he could afford to go and live in California for a year.

# 3.

# A Rake's Progress:
# America, 1964–67

Hockney's years at the RCA coincided with the birth of Swinging London and the liberated spirit of the 1960s. But he was always ambivalent about the expression and its claims of liberation, once remarking: 'Swinging Sixties meant miniskirts and all that; I would rather have had them showing less legs and keeping the pubs open a bit longer.' Even in an era of cultural revolution, London and England were too limiting: *Domestic Scene, Los Angeles* had shown where his desires lay.

Hockney left London for New York in December 1963. Here, he finished his *Rake's Progress* etchings – a group of sixteen plates, narrowed down from fifty. Touring the city with Jeff Goodman, he met Andy Warhol and other celebrities including the actor Dennis Hopper. A photograph taken by Hopper on the set of the TV drama *Naked City* shows Hockney, Goodman, Warhol and Henry Geldzahler, curator of twentieth-century art at the Metropolitan Museum, who was to be a lifelong friend. The image has all the saturnine allure of a gangster-movie still. Hockney frowns behind the twin orbs of his black-framed glasses; Goodman exhales a cloud of smoke; Warhol lurks slightly apart in the background – masked by sunglasses – and Geldzahler chomps on a cigar, the collar of his anorak tugged upwards.

But New York was to be no more than a stop-off. Hockney had a deep-seated sense that he would love California, which had sprung from his love of Hollywood films and from the pages of *Physique Pictorial*, the gay erotic publication disguised as a fitness and bodybuilding magazine. In photographs by Bob Mizer and his acolytes, purveyors of the 'beefcake' aesthetic of the mid-twentieth century, California held out a promise of rippling men, blue skies and shiny American brands. Hockney's preconceptions of Los Angeles had also been shaded by John Rechy's novel *City of Night* (1963), about a young hustler who travels there from New York.

Hockney flew out in January 1964. Four years later, he would recount how, as he flew over San Bernardino and looked down at the swimming pools in the back gardens, he was more thrilled than he had ever been arriving in a city. He stayed at the Tumble Inn Motel in Santa Monica and procured a bicycle. One of his first excursions was a cycle ride down Wilshire Boulevard to Pershing Square, the park in downtown Los Angeles that Rechy had mentioned as a spot for hustlers. It was an eighteen-mile trip: by the time he arrived, around nine in the evening, the place was deserted and there was nothing to do except drink a glass of beer.

Oliver Andrews, a sculptor with whom Hockney became friendly, advised him against cycling. In the first week after his arrival, he bought a Ford Falcon and passed his driving test. He also rented an apartment in Santa Monica and found a small studio in Venice – whose coastline boardwalk, with its roller skaters, he regarded as a sunny bare-fleshed version of Portobello Road. Another early outing was to Bob Mizer's studio to buy some stills. At the home of *Physique Pictorial*, he found a swimming pool with stained concrete sides, surrounded by plaster statues in a 'tacky' Grecian style. Mizer, who liked to declare, 'Remember, we are AMG [Athletic Model Guild], not MGM', was known for employing men off the street or straight out of the city jail to pose in faux-domestic scenarios.

The real enticements of Los Angeles quickly supplanted Hockney's fantasies. He fell in love with the city, which had both the energy of the United States and the picturesque elegance of the Mediterranean. Los Angeles was three times better, he later recalled, than he had expected it to be. It felt new – a city where everybody came from somewhere else. He loved the feeling of space: the vast expanse of the gridded streets and the desert beyond. Some of the freeways were still being built at the time: in his first week Hockney saw a ramp of freeway soaring into the air, which made him think that the city needed a Piranesi.

Hollywood was its own cultural centre, too – the Florence of the twentieth century. Los Angeles boasted a big gay bar, the Red Raven on Melrose Avenue, that was unlike anything in New York. And then there were the allures of the beach, with its pageant of beautiful bodies. In his first Californian paintings, Hockney translated the near-naked men of beefcake photoshoots into sleek domestic settings. *Boy About to Take a Shower* (1964), based on a Mizer photograph, shows a naked youth standing before the black-and-grey tiled wall of a shower, his lithe body abruptly pale around the buttocks. In *Man Taking Shower in Beverly Hills* (1964), a similarly built figure bends over beneath a torrent of spurting, dancing water. This latter piece was completed in Iowa during a six-week stint of teaching at the university.

Hockney's fascination with swimming pools, ignited by the view from the plane, can first be glimpsed in *California Art Collector* (1964). The work was painted in acrylics – a new discovery which allowed him to create a smooth, uniform and thin surface that perfectly suited the picture's ambience of suburban calm. A slender middle-aged woman in a green dress sits on a patterned armchair beneath a minimalist canopy, faced by two sculptures – an elongated head and an abstract stack of stones. In the background is the pristine turquoise oblong of a pool, bordered by palm trees.

The faintly surrealist tableau was inspired by Hockney's experiences of being invited to the homes of collectors and shown around by their wives. The open-walled house, and the attendant ambivalence between interior and exterior, are reminiscent of the Bailey House, popularly known as Case Study House #21, which was famously photographed by Julius Shulman in 1960. Hockney would later cite Shulman's photographs of this Modernist icon, along with *Physique Pictorial*, as his primary reason for coming to Los Angeles.

Years earlier, he had read the novels of Christopher Isherwood, the British writer who had emigrated to the US – along with W.H. Auden – in 1939. Before Hockney left London, the poet Stephen Spender had provided him with Isherwood's phone number. And so he called, and was invited to tea at the house in Santa Monica that Isherwood shared with his lover Don Bachardy, a young portrait artist. Isherwood had met Bachardy in 1952, on a stretch of beach visible from their living-room window. Hockney soon became a regular visitor. Isherwood declared at the time: 'Oh David, we've so much in common; we love California, we love American boys, and we're both from the north of England.'

On a return trip to London in December 1964, Hockney gave a talk at the Institute of Contemporary Art (ICA) at the invitation of Richard Hamilton. As a visiting artist to the RCA, Hamilton had been an early supporter of Hockney's, awarding him a prize that earned him new respect among the college's old guard. The subject of the ICA lecture was gay imagery in America. He showed slides of drawings by the graphic artist Tom of Finland, together with Super-8 silent films of men in soft-porn scenarios. A film titled *Leave my Ball Alone* featured a handsome youth discovering a version of the ancient Discobolus statue, holding a ball. When the youth tries to steal the ball, the statue comes alive and wrestles him in the nude.

In the summer of 1965, Hockney taught at the University of Colorado, Boulder, before returning to Los Angeles via the Colorado Goldmines, San Francisco and Disneyland. The following January, he travelled to Beirut, where he produced a group of thirteen etchings responding to the poems of Constantine Cavafy, to be published as part of a new translation by Stephen Spender and Nikos Stangos. This was Hockney's first major series of etchings since *A Rake's Progress*. His line drawings of daily life in Lebanon, which touched only obliquely on the seedy, melancholic atmosphere and Alexandrian setting of Cavafy's poems, instanced his growing tendency towards a sparing mode of realism.

Homoeroticism was at the fore of the images, too. Anonymous naked men are seen hooking up and lounging in bed. They slumber or gaze out with detached calm. Hockney has referred to the etchings as scenes of nonchalance in which the boys look out at the viewer unashamedly, almost insolently. When, in 1968, he met the elderly E.M. Forster – who had known Cavafy – and showed him his etchings, Forster remarked: 'They used not to show all that in my day.'

December 1965 saw Hockney's second show with Kasmin, *Pictures with Frames and Still-Life Pictures*, which included a number of recent works from America. Critics quickly realised that he had ceased to be a merely English painter. Writing in *Studio International*, Edward Lucie-Smith expressed double-edged admiration: 'Chameleon-like, he has become a Californian, and his art has taken on some of the characteristics of the environment ... The sardonic, humourless irony of the show makes him seem a more impressive if a less charming artist.'

In tandem with the Cavafy etchings, Hockney was working on designs for sets and costumes for a revival of Alfred Jarry's *Ubu Roi*, an absurdist comic drama first performed in 1896 in Paris. This was his first experience of working in the theatre. William Gaskill, the artistic director of the Royal Court, London, had invited him to work on the production. Initially reluctant, Hockney was drawn in by Jarry's subversive stage directions, which prohibited traditional scenery. He made a drawing of each scene, envisaging little painted backdrops that would be incongruously small compared with the stage.

In July 1966, Hockney opened his third solo show with Kasmin, which included both the Cavafy etchings and his theatre designs. The gallery had become a cultural beacon thanks to its trendsetting exhibitions and heady social ambience (painter Gillian Ayres once called it 'the place to be seen and the place to be shown') – and had been singled out, in April that year, in *Time* magazine's issue on 'Swinging London'. But Hockney's sights remained on America. Immediately after the opening, he returned to Los Angeles, where he had received an invitation to teach painting for a six-week summer school at UCLA. On Pico Boulevard, Santa Monica, he found a studio – a shabby converted garage.

Among Hockney's class at UCLA, which consisted mostly of Californian housewives, was a handsome boy with long brown-blond hair, the eighteen-year-old Peter Schlesinger. Almost instantly, Hockney was entranced. Schlesinger, who hailed from a strict Jewish background, took longer to reciprocate. But by the end of the summer, they had embarked on a love affair. For each of them, it was an awakening.

Hockney's first painting upon his return to California was a portrait of Betty Freeman, a collector, photographer and philanthropist who lived in Beverly Hills. He had begun by asking Freeman if he could come to her house to paint the swimming pool in her backyard. But he ended up creating a twelve-foot panorama showing Freeman at the centre of her pristine domestic world, based on black-and-white photographs. Freeman, who had been a prominent collector of Abstract Expressionist art throughout the 1950s, appears in the picture as a totem-straight figure in a long pink dress, standing in front of her glass-fronted house. Around her are attributes including a zebra-fur recliner by Le Corbusier and one of the stacked rock assemblages by sculptor William Turnbull that were *de rigueur* at the time. (The scene was to be recreated in Jack Hazan's biographical documentary film *A Bigger Splash*, in an episode where Schlesinger visits Freeman and swims in her pool.)

It was Freeman who proposed the painting's title, *Beverly Hills Housewife*, despite the fact that she was far more than a 'lady who lunches', having only recently abandoned her ambition to be a concert pianist. (She would become a formidable patron of modern music.) 'I had just given a small, private concert,' she recalled of this period, 'and it had gone very well, but I suddenly realized that was the best I would ever be. I closed the piano and never opened it again.' Hockney's portrait of Freeman at this moment of personal recalibration was to be the first in a grand sequence of high-precision interior scenes dating from between 1966 and 1974, many of them evoking the characters and habitats of well-to-do Los Angeles.

In six other paintings from 1966, he concentrated on the motif of the swimming pool, using photographs to create abstracted, simplified scenes of sunlit California. He was fascinated by the effects of light on water or glass – and the difficulty of capturing them pictorially. *Sunbather* shows a nude man – based on an illustration in a magazine – lying frontwards on a towel above an expanse of liquid blue overspread by serpentine lines. Next came *Portrait of Nick*

*Wilder*, which shows Hockney's Californian dealer emerging, head and shoulders, from his pool. The artist was staying with Wilder in West Hollywood at this time. *Peter Getting Out of Nick's Pool* depicts Peter Schlesinger, Hockney's new love, as he levers himself out of the same pool. As a reference, Hockney had taken a series of photographs of Schlesinger posing naked against the hood of his MG car, a hand on each front lamp. Schlesinger, who was by now training to be an artist at the University of California, Santa Cruz, had become Hockney's ideal model.

Towards the end of 1966, Hockney was browsing a newsstand in Hollywood when he came across a magazine called *Sunset Swimming Pools*, a guide to design and maintenance. It contained a photograph of an explosive splash. This marked the genesis of three paintings that would become icons of his career. *The Little Splash* took only two days to paint. *The Splash* was a six-foot-square painting that repeated the motif with more background detail – cacti on the poolside, a Modernist house, a slab of hillside. Hockney then painted *A Bigger Splash*, an eight-foot-square canvas in which the splash – which alone took two weeks to depict with fine brushes – bursts out of the rectilinear geometry of the pool, poolside, house and sky.

In January 1967, Schlesinger transferred from Santa Cruz to the University of California, Los Angeles. For six months, he lived with Hockney at the Pico Boulevard studio. Initially, he pretended to his parents that he was living somewhere else; when they learned the truth, they sent him to see a psychiatrist. Fortunately, the shrink sessions amounted to little more than casual gossiping. Wilder helped alleviate the situation by pointing out to Schlesinger's parents that the set-up was one of comparative stability: would they rather that he was hustling on Santa Monica Boulevard?

The living was basic, however, in that six-month period. Hockney's studio was the worst he ever lived in. The mere act of turning on the gas caused cockroaches to scuttle out of the oven. The absence of a phone required him to use the booth outside. And yet their life here was one of easy domesticity and prolific work – a hiatus from Hockney's restless roaming. Schlesinger would spend most of the day out at UCLA, and in the evenings they either stayed in (Schlesinger, who turned nineteen that April, was too young to venture out to bars) or saw friends. At the centre of their social world was Nick Wilder, with his parties filled with beautiful men, as well as Isherwood and Bachardy. Hockney recalled it later as his happiest year in Los Angeles.

In the spring of 1967, Hockney undertook a ten-week programme of teaching at Berkeley, close to San Francisco. It was in his large temporary studio at Berkeley that he completed *A Bigger Splash*, as well as *The Room, Tarzana* (1967) – an image of Schlesinger lying on his front on a bed, naked from his waist down to his socks (one of the first things Hockney had noticed about LA was that everybody wore little white socks), while light floods in from a window at the edge of the scene. The crisp green bedspread had been replicated from an advertisement for a 'pre-ironed for life' counterpane, while Schlesinger had posed by lying on a table. The title, referring to the neighbourhood of Tarzana in the San Fernando Valley, was a decoy.

Schlesinger was worried that his parents might see the picture and recognise him as its subject. The Schlesingers came from Encino, and so Hockney transferred the setting into another suburb, to mask the association.

In the summer, Hockney brought the painting to London, still unfinished, to show at Kasmin's gallery the following January. The real Schlesinger accompanied him (they sailed cabin class on the RMS *Queen Elizabeth*, a masterpiece of 'Dowdy Deco'), entering into the pattern of crossovers between California and Europe that would structure their existence over the next few years. From London, they toured Italy and France in the company of Patrick Procktor, a trip that coincided with Hockney's discovery of the 35mm camera. From this time on, he chronicled his life – and, in particular, his travels – in thousands of photographs, which he assembled in albums or 'diaries'.

In the medieval village of Carennac, France, Kasmin and his wife, Jane Nicholson, had rented a château with Howard Hodgkin. Hockney drew endlessly during the long, indolent days of the holiday – mostly sketches of Schlesinger. Other friends came and went, in a ritual that would also be repeated over many summers to come. Back at the flat on Powis Terrace, Hockney continued to make numerous pen-and-ink drawings of his lover, many of them recalling the languor and precision of his Cavafy series.

# 4.

# Double Portrait: Los Angeles, London and Beyond, 1968–71

When they returned to California in early 1968, Hockney and Schlesinger moved to a tiny penthouse in a 1930s apartment building in Santa Monica. Despite the smallness of his studio, Hockney determined to make a large-scale painting of his friends Christopher Isherwood and Don Bachardy. Along with *American Collectors (Fred & Marcia Wiseman)*, also painted in the early months of 1968, this marked the beginning of a series of double portraits.

Hockney took numerous photographs of Isherwood and Bachardy, and made preparatory drawings, but for the final picture he wanted to paint each of his friends from life. Having completed Isherwood, he took the rolled-up unfinished canvas to London, where Bachardy had decamped for two months, only to end up missing him. And so Bachardy's portrait was painted from photographs. The scene presents the two men in matching wicker armchairs – Isherwood turning to look at Bachardy, who in turn gazes out at the viewer – against the gentle variegated blues of their living-room shutters. In the foreground is a vast coffee table on which two stacks of books, mirroring the positions of the two men, rise on either side of a bowl of fruit and a desiccated cob of corn. Hockney had set up this 'still life' specially, ensuring that the light hit the objects just as he wanted.

In the summer of that year, Hockney relocated to London. Schlesinger had gained a place at the Slade School of Art – and was keener than Hockney to live in London. But the pair soon settled into a new rhythm at Powis Terrace. Schlesinger took a studio round the corner, and he set about transforming Hockney's scruffy, unloved flat into a stylish home – attending to curtains, tiles, furniture and antiques (as recorded in the 1972 short film *Portrait of David Hockney*, in which the camera lingers on the various small details of the living space). Hockney was both shocked and amused when, on one occasion, Schlesinger spent £750 on a leather sofa from Harrods.

Not long after arriving in London, Schlesinger joined Hockney on holiday in Le Nid du Duc, an abandoned hamlet in the hills above St Tropez belonging to the director Tony Richardson, whom Hockney had met during his work on *Ubu Roi*. The charismatic, capricious Richardson had staged John Osborne's *Look Back in Anger* at the Royal Court in 1956 and directed the film version two years later. The Provençal 'owl's nest', which Richardson had bought in 1965, became a favourite holiday destination of Hockney's, as well as a summertime mecca for artistic and literary stars of the era. The barrister and writer John Mortimer once observed that there seemed never to be fewer than twenty guests. These included Rudolf Nureyev, John Gielgud and Iris Murdoch.

In October 1968, Hockney met W.H. Auden, having been invited to draw him by the music critic of *The Observer*, Peter Heyworth. To Auden's annoyance, Hockney took R.B. Kitaj (his old RCA friend) and Schlesinger along with him, wrongly assuming, perhaps, that the poet would be pleased by the presence of a handsome young man. Auden made various barbed remarks about the manners of people who have no manners, in between generalised rants against the ubiquity of pornography. Hockney later wondered if he was playing a role. A photograph taken by Schlesinger shows the artist in a striped rugby shirt, bent over his sketchpad, while Auden stares grimly into the middle distance. Hockney made three drawings: two profile views and one frontal (which he later tore up). He reportedly remarked afterwards: 'I kept thinking, if Auden's face looks like this, what must his balls look like?' His drawings of Auden were among various portraits he made of gay writers and friends in these years, including Angus Wilson and Stephen Spender.

In the winter, Hockney embarked on a new double portrait, this time of Henry Geldzahler and his lover Christopher Scott. In preparation, he flew to New York and sketched the men in their apartment in the Wyoming Building on 7th Avenue. Geldzahler was at the height of his career at the Metropolitan Museum, preparing to stage the landmark exhibition *New York Painting and Sculpture: 1940–1970*. On the same trip, Hockney took the opportunity to pick up a variety of gay magazines from 42nd Street, including the idealistically billed *Golden Boys*, *Teenage Nudist* and *Naked Youth*.

As he passed through customs at London Heathrow, the officials decided that the publications were obscene, despite Hockney's insistence that they were to serve as artistic aids. Furious at their seizure, he resolved to take the case to court. He solicited the support of the art historian Kenneth Clark (who was willing to testify on his behalf) and Norman Reid, director of the Tate Gallery. News of the rising furore reached the ears of the Home Secretary, James Callaghan, and eventually the magazines were returned in a large brown envelope from HM Customs and Excise, labelled 'OHMS' (On Her Majesty's Service).

The completed picture of Geldzahler and Scott shows the former seated at the centre of a pink velvet sofa, meeting the viewer's eye, while Scott stands to one side, buttoned up in a raincoat as if he has just walked in from outside, watching his lover. Among the final touches were the highlights in Geldzahler's glasses and polished shoes. 'If I were Jan van Eyck,' Hockney remarked in an interview of May 1969, 'I'd put my whole picture in that little reflection.' The sofa was, in real life, a battered and unlovely object – the sleek pink upholstery was Hockney's invention. He spoke of the picture as St Henry radiating light, visited by Christopher Scott as an angel in an anorak.

For much of 1969, Hockney was engaged with a series of etchings themed around the fairy tales of the Brothers Grimm. By way of preparation, he had taken a trip down the Rhine the previous September, photographing the castles along the river and stopping at Colmar to view the Isenheim

Altarpiece. In the summer, he holidayed in France, visiting the spa town of Vichy. His photographs include shots of Schlesinger reading Proust in their hotel, and of a park in which Schlesinger and Ossie Clark sit in plastic chairs in front of an avenue of trees, turned away from the camera. A third plastic chair, placed to one side of them, suggests Hockney's own vacated seat. In January 1970, Hockney would begin the grand-scaled *Le parc des sources, Vichy*, reproducing this scene – and the strange effect of the triangle of trees, which had been planted to exaggerate the impression of receding perspective. Along with his concurrent painting of Ossie Clark and Celia Birtwell, it marked the high point of his experiment with high-precision naturalism and one-point perspective.

In November 1969, Hockney had his first exhibition at the New York gallery of André Emmerich. This included his three double portraits, *Christopher Isherwood and Don Bachardy*, *Henry Geldzahler and Christopher Scott*, and *American Collectors*. Emmerich was a suave, soft-spoken Manhattan dealer who had achieved renown in the 1950s as a champion of Colour Field painting. His programme came to include painters – such as Hockney – who didn't fit the post-war abstract mould, although that diversification didn't please everyone in his rarefied circle. Clement Greenberg, the renowned Modernist art critic who had influenced the dealer's early proclivity for abstract painters, was heard muttering at Hockney's exhibition: 'This is not art for a serious gallery.'

Shortly afterwards, a retrospective of Hockney's paintings and works on paper was held at the Whitechapel Art

Gallery in London. Organised by Mark Glazebrook, it was the first survey of his work, and comprised forty-five paintings and forty-seven drawings. Hockney was now thirty-two. The show was a dazzling accolade, and yet the experience of seeing a decade's worth of work was somewhat deflating – perhaps oppressive. During the hanging, he stayed away at Le Nid du Duc with Isherwood and Schlesinger, returning just in time for the private view. Friends reported that he was bemused by the display and kept saying: 'How protean art is.'

Unfinished at the time of the Whitechapel exhibition was the large double portrait of his friends Celia Birtwell and Ossie Clark that Hockney had worked on for much of the previous year. Birtwell and Clark were collaborators and leading lights of the fashion world – she created prints for his clothes designs at the Quorum boutique in Chelsea. They had married in 1969, with Hockney as best man, although their marriage (which probably only occurred at the prompting of Birtwell's father, because she was pregnant) was to be short-lived. Clark was hedonistic, promiscuous and occasionally violent. As he veered away from his wife, however, she became increasingly close to Hockney.

The painting was finally completed in February 1971. In contrast to the earlier double portraits, where one subject looks at the other, each of the figures gazes out serenely at the viewer. The scene is the Clarks' flat in Notting Hill, although much of it was executed in Hockney's Powis Terrace studio. Clark lounges in a chair, his feet buried in the deep shagpile carpet which Hockney had introduced in the course of painting, unable to get Clark's feet right. A white cat perches on his thigh – named Blanche in real life, but rechristened Percy (after the couple's other cat) in the title of the painting. Birtwell stands on the other side of the window in a plunging caftan, one of Clark's designs. On the wall is an etching from Hockney's *Rake's Progress* series: *Meeting the Good People*. Through the window, bright sunlight irradiates the stucco terrace across the street.

The composition would become one of the most recognisable in Hockney's oeuvre. It developed out of numerous photographs and sketches, as well as long sittings. The short film *Portrait of David Hockney* (1972) shows Birtwell – who was pregnant at the time with her second child – dreamily observing the artist as he paints her into the scene, starting with a sparing outline of her face and body. Clark was a less attentive sitter. His love of nightclubbing interfered with daytime sessions, and his face had to be repainted around twelve times. According to some accounts, the painting was intended as a late wedding present. Clark later recounted having sold it for £7,000, although Hockney's biographer Christopher Simon Sykes has identified this as a piece of retrospective mythmaking – the painting Clark sold was a different one entirely.

By this time, Hockney was travelling more than ever, taking a foreign trip at least once a month and obsessively photographing his experiences. Snapshots taken at Le Nid du Duc in 1969 include images of him and Patrick Procktor playing chess, and various guests lounging around the pool that Hockney would make famous in his painting *Portrait of an Artist (Pool with Two Figures)* (1972). Over the course of 1970, he filled some eight albums with travel pictures.

In March 1971, in an effort to escape their hectic and increasingly fractious life in London, Hockney and Schlesinger travelled to Marrakech with Celia Birtwell. Hockney was enchanted by the gardens of La Mamounia hotel. He wrote to Henry Geldzahler that the place was rather like the Beverly Hills Hotel, only more Moroccan. He made various drawings of Schlesinger, including one in which the younger man gazes out from their balcony at the city.

Back in London, Hockney began work on *Sur la terrasse*, a vast painting showing Schlesinger on their balcony at La Mamounia, viewed from behind through an open door. Based dually on a photograph and a crayon sketch, the scene is cast in brilliant, preternatural light: turquoise shadows stream across the white floor; Peter's pink shirt and tight white trousers glow against a green haze of palm trees.

But the image testifies, more than anything, to the growing distance between them. Schlesinger was feeling constrained by their life at Powis Terrace – and frustrated by his inability to step out of Hockney's shadow. He had also begun to fall in love with a young photography and fashion student at the RCA, Eric Boman. As Boman began to turn up daily at Powis Terrace, Hockney turned a blind eye, convincing himself that it was nothing more than a passing fling. But the writing was on the wall for their five-year relationship.

After Morocco, Hockney left Schlesinger in London and went to New York and California for three weeks. He made a drawing of Robert Mapplethorpe, who was living with Patti Smith, later to find fame as a rock musician, at the Chelsea Hotel. Mapplethorpe gave him a Polaroid of a male nude, although at that time he was pursuing sculpture more than photography: Hockney and Mo McDermott paid a visit to his studio a few days later, where they saw a variety of leather-clad crosses and stars. When Hockney returned to London, Schlesinger announced that he was leaving for Paris. It was at this moment that Hockney accepted, with anguish, that Schlesinger was in love with someone else. Schlesinger left, and Hockney continued work on *Sur la terrasse*.

Not long after, Hockney received a visit from Jack Hazan, a filmmaker who had come across a copy of the catalogue from the Whitechapel retrospective. Hazan wanted to make a film about Hockney's life. This, he claimed, would be a new kind of art film – a witty, ironic take on the painter's existence. Despite Hockney's misgivings, Hazan persuaded him: Hockney later claimed that he had agreed to do the film just to stop Hazan from 'nattering' at him (in the Yorkshire sense of 'complaining' or 'pestering') on the phone. For the next three years, Hazan followed the artist intermittently around the world.

Hockney's relationship with Schlesinger came decisively to an end in August, while they were on holiday in Carennac with the Kasmins and other friends including Mo McDermott, Wayne Sleep, George Lawson, Ossie Clark and Celia Birtwell. Schlesinger wanted to travel up to Cadaqués in Spain, where their friend Mark Lancaster had rented an apartment. Unaware of the situation, Lancaster had also invited Eric Boman to stay. Hockney and Schlesinger ended up in a screaming match on the dock at Cadaqués, where Schlesinger had wanted to attend a boat party, before

Hockney drove away in fury. Back in Carennac, he was overcome with remorse and decided to drive all the way back to Cadaqués – a five-hour trip – only for Schlesinger to tell him that he didn't want him there.

The end of the relationship was agonising for Hockney. After their holiday showdown, Schlesinger moved out of Powis Terrace. Lonely and depressed, Hockney threw himself into his work, painting for up to fifteen hours a day. He began smoking again, having stopped at Schlesinger's request. The crisis coincided with a painting, begun in late October, that would ultimately be called *Portrait of an Artist* – the last of his seminal pool paintings. The composition showed Schlesinger standing in a suit at the end of a swimming pool, watching as a figure swims underwater towards him. Hockney had happened to juxtapose two unrelated photographs on his studio floor to create the structure of the image: an underwater swimmer (taken in 1966 in Hollywood) and a man staring at the ground.

The fraught progress of this work forms a memorable sequence in Hazan's film, *A Bigger Splash*. In April, only weeks before the painting's planned exhibition at André Emmerich Gallery, and after multiple reworkings, Hockney decided that the perspective and form of the figure in the pool were wrong – and he resolved to start again. Kasmin told him he was mad. Hockney took a two-day trip to Le Nid du Duc and staged the composition afresh, with Mo McDermott modelling as the standing figure, and John St Clair – a young photographer – swimming underwater. St Clair dived repeatedly into the pool before finally cracking his head on the bottom.

Back at his studio, Hockney made a further revision: unhappy with the photographs of McDermott taken in France, he went with Schlesinger to Kensington Gardens (though separated, the two were still on speaking terms) and took a new round of photographs, in which Schlesinger stands at the edge of a path. And so the final picture, which is often grouped with the Californian pool paintings, was really a conflation of Provence and west London. For two weeks, Hockney worked for eighteen hours a day on the painting, taking advantage of Hazan's daylight-simulating equipment. The painting was finished and varnished one day before the deadline, and flown to New York rolled up. Henry Geldzahler interpreted the work, and in particular its title, as a form of letting go: 'David is giving Peter his birthright … he's calling him an artist. It's very difficult to have your progeny learn to fly.'

# 5.

# David by David:
# London and Paris, 1972–76

For six months, Hockney worked on a large double portrait of the dancer Wayne Sleep and his partner, George Lawson, an antiquarian book dealer. Hockney had met Lawson through Kasmin, and had immediately warmed to his camp sense of humour. Lawson and Sleep had themselves met at a party of Kasmin's, after which Sleep had moved into Lawson's flat on Wigmore Place in Marylebone. Hockney's painting shows Sleep watching his lover from a doorway, while Lawson sits at a miniature clavichord and plays a single note. The work was originally to have the punning title *A Flat*.

Back in London after his opening in New York, Hockney found himself struggling with this composition, in particular the gradation of light across the large bare wall. Kasmin wanted it for his final exhibition before closing his Bond Street gallery at the end of 1972, having decided to pursue private dealing. But Hockney refused to let him have it. Acrylic paint, and the high naturalistic style he had mastered using it, had come to feel more than ever a dead end. Lawson has speculated that Hockney was impaired more by the turmoil of his break-up than by technical challenges:

'The problem wasn't really the vanishing point, it was the vanishing Peter.' The unfinished painting would remain rolled up for decades before Hockney decided to donate it to Tate Britain in 2014.

Kasmin's final show featured works inspired by a fortnight-long trip Hockney had made to Japan shortly after the break-up with Schlesinger – for instance, *Mount Fuji and Flowers* (1972), a vase of white jonquils viewed on a ledge in front of a rendering of the mountain in deep-blue washes. The critic Guy Brett drily remarked in *The Times* that Hockney 'has been exercising … without much to say', and that the paintings 'lack his customary edge'.

Early in 1973, Hockney left London for Los Angeles. Staying at the Chateau Marmont hotel – famous by then as a celebrity hangout – he produced a number of lithographs at the suggestion of Ken Tyler and Sid Felsen of the Gemini Press. Themed around different aspects of the weather, these mimicked the crisp stylisation of Japanese art. *Sun* was a still life based on a view in Isherwood and Bachardy's house: rays of light streak across a plant positioned in front of blue shutters.

Hockney's great companion and muse at this time was Celia Birtwell, whose marriage to Ossie Clark – never stable – was falling apart, with Clark disappearing for days at a time on drug-fuelled misadventures. She came with her two boys to stay with Hockney in February at his rented house in Malibu. Here he made further lithographic works including three large portraits of her. She and Hockney became intensely close, sometimes sleeping in the same bed, although the relationship was never sexual. 'I was a good listener,' she said in an interview in 2020, 'and that's really how he got to know me. You always need someone to talk to about what's in your heart, and I think I played that role.' In the end, Clark turned up with a bagful of drugs and persuaded Birtwell to come away with him to Palm Springs.

That summer, Hockney went travelling with a friend from New York, Joe MacDonald. Square-jawed and muscular, MacDonald was emerging as the first male supermodel. While they were in Geneva, Jack Hazan turned up and filmed a conversation between the two friends in a hotel room: a slow mirthful interchange about when, exactly, Hockney had decided MacDonald was artistic. This dialogue would form the opening and closing sequences of *A Bigger Splash* (1974), and would take on a heightened retrospective poignancy after MacDonald's death from AIDS in 1983.

In Avignon, Hockney saw an exhibition of Picasso's late work together with the art scholar and collector Douglas Cooper. Picasso's death earlier that year had deeply moved Hockney, who had long felt an affinity with the Modernist master, even though they had never met. Cooper, who had been to see the show before, dismissed the paintings as geriatric daubings. But Hockney insisted on looking more carefully. While some of the paintings seemed slapdash, he realised that few other artists have achieved the freedom that Picasso did at the end of his life, varying wildly in subject and style.

In August, Hockney and Henry Geldzahler rented the villa of art critic Mario Amaya, close to Lucca in Italy, to work on a book together (the project never saw publication). After two weeks, Kasmin turned up – fresh from a heated row with his estranged wife – along with two friends. One of these was Eugene Lambe, an eccentric Irishman whom the poet Derek Mahon would later remember as 'colloquial yet ornate, one of those perfect writers who never write'. Hockney made a sketch of Lambe in colouring pencils, in which he appears as a pale, enigmatic character with a long red beard. Dressed in a broad-brimmed panama and loose blue shirt, he is caught in a moment of reflection or abstraction. Hockney called the drawing *Dr Eugen Lamb*, misspelling his subject's name and conferring on him an imaginary academic title that seemed to befit his professorial air. On an excursion to Florence, Hockney also sketched Michelangelo's *David*, annotating the drawing 'David by David'. He and Geldzahler dined at the sumptuous Florence home of Harold Acton, who had been a model for the character of Anthony Blanche in Evelyn Waugh's *Brideshead Revisited* (1945).

At the end of September, still haunted by the break-up with Schlesinger, Hockney moved to Paris. He was in his mid-thirties and internationally successful, but he felt trapped by the dead end of his own 'obsessive naturalistic' style, and wanted space and time to experiment. He rented a flat from his friend Tony Richardson on the Cour de Rohan. The sequestered building, coated in ivy and accessed via iron gates, had once been the Palace of the Bishops of Rohan, and more recently had housed the studio of the French painter Balthus. Paris offered a liberating break from the social whirlwind of London life. Hockney was able to paint for eight hours a day uninterrupted. Not knowing the French language allowed him to feel detached. He lived quietly, spending much time in the Louvre or the Musée d'Art Moderne, or sitting in cafés, when he wasn't working. He started each morning in the café at the top of his street, where he drank tea and ate 'delicious bread and butter'. In the early evening, he walked to the Café de Flore where he usually met someone he knew.

In Paris, Hockney felt sequestered not only from his old life but from the contemporary art world, then under the sway of minimalism and conceptualism. 'Contemporary art I felt quite removed from,' he later wrote. 'The rise of conceptualism had made it all rather arid to me, utterly unsensual and alien … One forgets how small an art world is, or how many art worlds there are.'

From late 1973 into 1974, Hockney worked with the master printmaker Aldo Crommelynck, a tall, gaunt figure with nicotine-stained fingers who had produced Picasso's prints for twenty years, to create a number of etchings. They had already worked together on a portfolio of prints commemorating Picasso the previous year; these included *The Student: Homage to Picasso*, in which Hockney depicted himself, quizzical and bow-tied, regarding a giant bust of the Spanish artist. His sequence of etchings *Contre-jour in the French Style* employed a pointillist technique to depict a single window in the Louvre, its blind half-closed to permit a fractional glimpse of the Tuileries Garden outside.

Hockney's social world may have contracted for a time, but connections with individual friends remained as vital as ever. Celia Birtwell visited continuously – she appears in many of his drawings from this period. New friends included Jean Léger (a designer; Hockney liked to claim that he worked in a lipstick factory), Gregory Evans and

Yves-Marie Hervé. The latter, 'Yves-Marie de Paris' as he was called, became Hockney's lover for a time. A pencil drawing of 1974 shows him curled up and lynx-like, with a sweep of dark hair over one eye. ('He was desirable,' according to Kasmin, 'even if you weren't gay.') Evans, who had grown up in Tulsa, Oklahoma, and escaped to San Francisco at the age of fifteen, had been the boyfriend of Nick Wilder, Hockney's Californian dealer. After breaking up with Wilder, he had come to live in Paris, arriving at the same time as Hockney.

Hockney's various studies of his friends were part of his attempt, at this time, to escape the trap of naturalism. He was almost moved to return to drawing skeletons, as he had done in his first week at the RCA. Drawing from life, often using colouring pencils, he worked with painstaking slowness and precision. 'I was trying to break out of something,' he admitted afterwards, 'break out of what I called obsessive naturalism. It took me a long time, when I think about it.'

Hockney also drew his old friend Andy Warhol, after Warhol came to Paris in December 1973. In return, Warhol took multiple photographs of Hockney. These formed the basis for three works titled *Portrait of David Hockney* (1974), silkscreen and acrylic paintings in which the artist's non-plussed visage emerges from a haze of pink or green or blue acrylic wash. Two of the paintings were gifts to Hockney; Warhol kept the third.

In his second year in Paris, Hockney returned to painting in oils. He was still using acrylics, however, when he produced a large double portrait of Shirley Goldfarb and Gregory Masurovsky, a pair of expatriate American artists. Goldfarb was a well-known figure at the Café de Flore, identifiable by her beatnik clothes and Yorkshire terrier. She and Masurovsky had lived for twenty years in two tiny adjoining studios. Hockney was fascinated by their living quarters and eccentric relationship – by the fact that Masurovsky couldn't leave the building without Goldfarb seeing, whereas she could depart unnoticed. He rendered their adjacent spaces in the style of a theatre set: one wall has been removed to allow a 'cross-section' view, with an imaginary rail and curtain forming a minimalist proscenium arch around the scene.

At the start of 1974, Jack Hazan invited Hockney to London to watch the completed *A Bigger Splash*. The film was a two-hour dramatisation of his life, centred on his break-up with Schlesinger, shot in a languorous and episodic style. Across a chain of discontinuous moments, the artist is seen chatting with friends, travelling to New York, and working alone at home in London. The action is interspliced with dream-like interludes: four naked youths swim in a sunlit pool, and at one moment Schlesinger wanders naked in the gardens of Los Angeles houses, not unlike the roaming protagonist of John Cheever's 1964 story 'The Swimmer'.

At the private screening, Hockney was aghast. He felt that he and his friends had been deceived. The presentation of his break-up with Peter – intense and yet highly mannered – was more than he could bear. Despite its *vérité* style, the film included various fictional insertions, such as the suggestion that he had cut up the first version of *Portrait of an Artist* in a fit of frustration, or the pretence that he had disappeared without trace during a trip to New York. (This was a *film noir* flourish: Hockney had actually gone on holiday to

France.) Several friends took a different view. Ossie Clark insisted: 'David, you can't ignore this film, it's truer than the truth.' Shirley Goldfarb persuaded him against trying to block the release. Nonetheless, he refused to attend a public screening in Cannes, despite the fact that he was staying nearby at Le Nid du Duc.

Others objected on more prudish grounds. The film's explicit gay content, including a long sequence in which Peter makes love with a friend, created obstacles in terms of distribution. The London Film Festival billed *A Bigger Splash* as their headline screening for 1974, before the director of the festival backtracked, having decided that the content was inappropriate for such a starring role, and moved it to the less prominent slot of the festival's closing night. In Paris, the film was initially banned for four months.

In the summer of 1974, Hockney had received an invitation to design a new production of Igor Stravinsky's 1951 opera *The Rake's Progress* (whose libretto had been penned by W.H. Auden and Chester Kallman), scheduled for the Glyndebourne Festival Opera the following year. The director, John Cox, had seen his designs for *Ubu Roi* at the Royal Court in 1966, and was also familiar with the *Rake's Progress* etchings of 1961–63.

The story and the words of the opera were what first attracted Hockney. Only after he had listened to the music ten times did he begin to love it. He started work on an elaborate scheme of sets and costumes, based on William Hogarth's original paintings and engravings charting the decline and fall of a young man who squanders his wealth and ends up in Bedlam. Hockney and Mo McDermott travelled to Los Angeles, where Stravinsky had composed the music, and checked into the Chateau Marmont hotel to work on the project. For McDermott, the trip was an act of penance – and enforced rest and recuperation. He had stolen and drunk all of the fine French wine from Powis Terrace (bought on trips to Burgundy with John Kasmin) while Hockney was away in Paris. He was also succumbing to heroin addiction, and had begun stealing drawings from Hockney in order to sell them.

Over the course of the year, Hockney had grown increasingly close to Gregory Evans. Polaroids taken in Paris in 1974–75 of Evans in the nude testify to their new intimacy. On a trip to Rome at the end of 1974, Hockney drew him among the ruins of the Palatine Hill; in one, he appears wrapped in a long anorak, gazing moodily over the top of a broken column. In a sign of the seriousness of the relationship, Hockney took Evans back to Yorkshire to meet his family, on the occasion of his aunt Rebecca's ('Aunt Rebe') eightieth birthday. (Yorkshire, Evans recalled, 'didn't feel to me that different in spirit to Kansas … It was dark and full of Gothic gloom.') Hockney would even allow a British gay magazine called *Playguy* to publish Polaroids of himself, Evans and a friend, all naked at the Paris flat. 'David Hockney's Private Nude Snaps!' was the line blazoned across the cover in January 1976.

A more solemn affirmation of Hockney's status had been the exhibition, opening in autumn 1974 at the Musée des Arts Décoratifs in the Louvre, of some thirty paintings and one hundred drawings. The focus was on recent work, and the catalogue contained an introduction by Stephen

Spender which sited Hockney in the alternative stream of English painting and poetry, along with William Blake. Praising his recent crayon drawings, the British critic Michael Ratcliffe wrote of 'the exuberance and economy with which he has taken the child's scribbling toy and transformed it'; Hockney's crayon portraits of his friends, above all of Celia Birtwell, were 'the crowning sophisticated glory of the Paris show'.

On 21 June 1975, the premiere of *A Rake's Progress* took place at the Glyndebourne Festival. The three-act opera featured backdrops and costumes festooned with cross-hatching in imitation of Hogarth's engravings. One hundred and fifty guests were treated to a celebratory dinner at a table running the length of the Glyndebourne ha-ha, organised by the gregarious (and famously bibulous) restaurateur Peter Langan. Hockney designed a cover for each of the menus, featuring drawings of Langan and his wine merchant. Over the top, Langan wrote 'An Evening of Excess'.

Hogarth was also the inspiration behind Hockney's painting *Kerby (After Hogarth) Useful Knowledge* (1975). In this unreal amalgam of viewpoints and figures, he was quoting Hogarth's frontispiece to a publication of 1754, *Dr Brook Taylor's Method of Perspective Made Easy* (by the artist and theorist Joshua Kirby), which he had come across while researching his opera designs. In Hogarth's engraving – a satire on the misuses of perspective – Hockney perceived a new source of liberation. The use of 'reverse perspective' – whereby the perspective lines in the picture converge towards the viewer, in defiance of the Renaissance ideal – would become a recurring feature of Hockney's subsequent work.

In the summer, Henry Geldzahler introduced Hockney to Fire Island, the gay haven off Long Island. They spent a month here, entranced by the place. Everybody was gay, Hockney recalled later, even the police, and anything went. Photographs taken by Robert Mapplethorpe show Hockney lounging and yawning on a wooden platform at the home of Bruce Mailman, a theatre owner. He took many photos of his own, filling a whole album. Hockney would return to Fire Island the following summer, when Geldzahler introduced him to Wallace Stevens's book-length poem, *The Man with the Blue Guitar* (1937), inspiring a portfolio of etchings conveying the poem's rhythms and imagery. Stevens had based the work on Picasso's *The Old Guitarist* (1903–04). Hockney was intrigued by the lines about 'a blue guitar' and the guitarist's refusal to 'play things as they are', which made him think of Picasso's refusal to paint things as they are.

After his first summer on Fire Island, Hockney went back to Paris. But the city had lost the appeal it had held for him two years earlier. He had never got to grips with speaking French. In addition, he was beginning to go deaf, an affliction inherited from his father: during French lessons, he had realised that he wasn't able to hear the teacher. His celebrity had risen in the wake of the Louvre show, and his apartment, once a haven, was now frequently overrun with visitors, just as Powis Terrace had been in the days of his thronging tea parties. People would arrive in the middle of the afternoon and hang around until midnight.

Hockney returned to London in November 1975. He had got rid of Powis Terrace, with all its associations of life with Schlesinger, and he now moved into a studio in Pembroke

Gardens, Kensington. At the start of the following year, he spent two weeks travelling across America with Evans. They stayed at various hotels, ranging from low-grade motels to the shabby splendour of the Arlington in Hot Springs, Arkansas, Frank Lloyd Wright's Biltmore Hotel in Phoenix, and finally a penthouse suite at the Chateau Marmont in Los Angeles. They then flew to Australia for an exhibition of Hockney's graphic work – his first visit to the country, where two of his brothers, Philip and John, had emigrated in 1961 and 1968 respectively. Afterwards, Evans returned to Paris and Hockney headed back to LA.

Here, he worked on a portfolio of etchings for the Gemini Press. These comprised portraits of friends such as Isherwood and Bachardy – in an image that reverses the poses of their earlier portrait – and Billy Wilder. Hockney's portrait of the legendary film director captures him at the age of sixty-nine, seated in a fold-up chair, a script resting between his hands and his lap. Wilder, who had engineered a meeting with Hockney some years earlier – and whose films *Sunset Boulevard* and *Some Like It Hot* Hockney had adored as a young man – returns the artist's gaze with a fond, quizzical expression. Hockney and Wilder were both regulars at a local restaurant where, as Hockney was later fond of recounting, the customers would stand and applaud when Wilder walked in.

Back in England in the summer of 1976, Hockney visited his family in Bradford – where his father, having discovered Christian Science, had neglected his diabetes with dire consequences for his mental and physical health. In London, he met up with Isherwood and Bachardy, who were over from LA for a month. The friends embarked on a hectic midsummer drive through the UK, during which they stopped in Aldeburgh, Suffolk, for dinner with Benjamin Britten and Peter Pears – in addition to numerous other sites and fixtures, including (on the final day of the tour) tea back in Bradford with Laura Hockney.

Isherwood and Bachardy were not the only recurring American characters in Hockney's life at this time. When an interviewer from *Gay News* visited Pembroke Gardens later that year, he came across Peter Schlesinger hanging around the studio and garden, waiting for Hockney to accompany him to a friend's for dinner. It was a testament, perhaps, to the openness and elasticity of his relationship with Gregory Evans that Hockney felt free to admit – when asked if his liaison with Schlesinger was still sexual – 'No. I would like it that way, but I can understand his point of view a bit. … I think it was Bernard Shaw who said "the single-minded should stay single".' He went on to admit that artists always put their work ahead of relationships ('very few artists actually had a good relationship with a close person').

October 1976 was the occasion of the publication of Hockney's autobiography, *David Hockney by David Hockney: My Early Years*, edited by Nikos Stangos. The book was launched at the Cartwright Hall in Bradford, followed by a string of events in London. It was widely acclaimed, and yet Hockney recoiled from the publicity. He was missing Evans – who was still in Paris – and felt understimulated. As in the mid-1960s, his thoughts were gravitating away from England.

# 6.
# Thoughts of Return: The Hollywood Hills, 1977–80

For the cover of the *New Review* magazine in January 1977, Hockney and his old friend R.B. Kitaj posed in the nude. In the black-and-white photograph, they stand side by side, as frontal and rigid as ancient Greek *kouroi*. Hockney has one arm around the shoulder of Kitaj, who – in contrast to his friend's unalloyed nakedness – wears a skimpy vest. The shot was taken for a dare by restaurateur Peter Langan, who happened to be sitting for Hockney at the time: details of the artist's studio can be glimpsed behind the improvised cardboard backdrop in front of which they pose. Along the bottom corner of the cover runs the tagline 'A Double Issue'.

In an interview inside the magazine, both artists defended figurative painting in vigorous terms. Even so, Hockney had been struggling for some time with his own mode of figuration. In 1975, while in Paris, he had attempted a portrait of his parents, before finding himself once more unable to outgrow the naturalistic style of his previous double portraits. This abandoned piece, in which the artist's own face appears in a mirror between his seated parents, remained in his Los Angeles home before finally being exhibited at the National Portrait Gallery in London in 2020, with masking tape still fixed to the surface. He had destroyed an even earlier version completely.

In 1977, he tried again. The resulting painting, completed that summer, shows his father engrossed in a book while his mother – seated on the other side of a wheelable trolley – looks out serenely at the artist and the viewer. Hockney has disappeared from the mirror, which instead reflects a fragment of the studio wall (including, in a wry touch, the corner of the previous abandoned canvas). The painting is an understated yet potent expression of the couple's dual distance and interdependence; for some years, Kenneth's profound deafness and failing health had inflicted strain on their relationship. 'I am sure he never heard a word my mother said for the last 10 years of his life, because she spoke so softly,' Hockney later reflected. Kenneth, who struggled to keep still during the sittings, is shown reading *Art and Photography* by Aaron Scharf, which makes reference to the use of the *camera obscura* in the Renaissance, anticipating Hockney's own theories in his book *Secret Knowledge* (2001).

By this time, Hockney had moved from Pembroke Gardens to a larger studio, having bought the top floor of 17 Powis Terrace (using the money from the sale of his old flat there). Here, he painted another portrait of his former lover, *Peter Schlesinger with a Polaroid Camera*. Schlesinger sat for a week for the picture. Dandyishly attired in a lilac suit, and yet arrestingly solemn, he is shown seated on a soft, chequered-fabric chair opposite a camera on a tripod. Six years after *Portrait of an Artist*, the painting was another kind of valediction – and a sign, possibly, of Hockney's struggle to let go. It was made just before Schlesinger moved to New York to live with Eric Boman.

Schlesinger appears more obliquely in another work from 1977, *Model with Unfinished Self-Portrait*. This shows Gregory Evans lying asleep in a blue robe in front of an incomplete painting of Hockney sitting in his studio, *Self-Portrait with Blue Guitar* (the resulting illusion is of the artist working behind his sleeping lover). But the feet are Schlesinger's – Evans had left again for Paris before Hockney could paint his feet, in a telling sign of his intermittence in the artist's life. 'After David went back to London, our relationship was ongoing, but it wasn't exclusive,' Evans told Christopher Simon Sykes, Hockney's biographer, in 2010. 'I had other relationships and also freedom to go where I wanted to go when I wanted to go.' In July, Hockney repeated the conceit of the 'painting within a painting' in *Looking at Pictures on a Screen*, a portrait of Henry Geldzahler. The curator stands looking at four reproductions of paintings by old and modern masters from the National Gallery in London: Vermeer, Piero della Francesca, Van Gogh and Degas – an index of Hockney's inspirations. Geldzahler, he once said, was 'one of the few people I talk about art a lot to'.

When the painting of his parents was unveiled at the Hayward Gallery in July, Kenneth and Laura were photographed on either side of it, with Hockney seated on the floor in between. Full of pride in her son, Laura was nonetheless put off by the austere architecture of the gallery, which she noted was 'very depressing'. The exhibition, which also featured Hockney's *Blue Guitar* etchings suite, *Self-Portrait with Blue Guitar* (1977), and *Model with Unfinished*

*Self-Portrait*, was the second part of the Hayward Annual, the inaugural edition of a series of contemporary exhibitions intended 'to present a cumulative picture of British art as it develops'. Curator Michael Compton, speaking on behalf of the selection committee (which also included Howard Hodgkin and William Turnbull), freely professed that the display was 'flagrantly partial'. From a present-day perspective, it is the absence of female artists that seems most flagrant – although this was redressed the following year by an all-women selection committee.

For Hockney, the Annual represented a battleground in the ongoing crisis in the visual arts – hinted at in the *New Review* interview – between traditionalists and the avant-garde. During the run of the exhibition, he took part in an edition of *Robbie*, the weekly television programme fronted by broadcaster Fyfe Robertson. In this, he sided enthusiastically with Robertson's withering view of the more experimental works on display, specifically Bob Law's abstract paintings and Stuart Brisley's performances, which Robertson considered 'phoney art'. In a public debate at the Hayward on 5 September, Hockney restated his views in the face of reprisals from Michael Compton. Robertson, less resilient, was driven from the room in tears. In 1979, Hockney would resume his attack on the elitism of artworld tastes: in an article for *The Observer* titled 'No Joy at the Tate' (4 March), he attacked the Tate Gallery's acquisitions policy under the directorship of Norman Reid, 'so biased in favour of joyless and soulless and theoretical art'.

In August 1977, Hockney and Evans stayed with Jane Kasmin and her two sons in the Alpine resort of Balme.

Hockney spent much of the holiday lying on the grass, listening to Mozart's *The Magic Flute* on the stereo of his parked car. Following the triumph of *The Rake's Progress*, John Cox at Glyndebourne had invited him to design a production of Mozart's opera for 1978. After the holiday, Evans went on to Spain to stay with a friend for four months. Reluctant to be alone in London, Hockney left for New York, where he immersed himself in his designs for *The Magic Flute*. New York, then in its hedonistic heyday, offered a release: Hockney went around with his friend Joe MacDonald, visiting gay hangouts such as Ramrod, a leather bar on the Hudson River waterfront.

For the opera's Egyptian setting, he took inspiration from various sources: the stylised depictions of Egypt in Renaissance art, the Egyptian collections at the Metropolitan Museum, and his own trips to Egypt. His first visit in 1963 had resulted in the painting *Great Pyramid at Giza with Broken Head from Thebes* – the first work, incidentally, in which he painted a palm tree. In 1978, he went again in the company of Joe MacDonald and Peter Schlesinger: the trio had joined a touring party made up of middle-aged couples and some pyramidologists from Tennessee. MacDonald and Schlesinger initially looked upon the rest of the group with good-humoured disdain, until Hockney reprimanded them for their snobbery. He carried with him a stash of guidebooks including a Baedeker from 1910. Sitting by the Nile, he was overcome by a sense of the vastness of historical time. The Islamic art of Cairo, too, was a revelation.

Hockney had decided, by this time, to make Los Angeles his permanent home once more. The experience of working with bold colours and simple, clear-cut shapes made him certain that his art would take a new direction when he returned to California after the production of *The Magic Flute.*

The opera premiered at Glyndebourne at the end of May 1978. Hockney's thirty-five backdrops received rapturous acclaim, and yet certain isolated criticisms hit home, including suggestions that his staging was a pastiche of Art Deco, or merely a stream of references to his own earlier output. These detractions only increased his eagerness to leave England as soon as possible. He wrote to Kitaj: 'The thought of spending all my future days in Powis Terrace fills me with horror, I would prefer a shack on Pico Blvd with beautiful flesh nearby.' He left Powis Terrace, and London, on 7 August.

On his way to California, he stopped off in New York. He was invited upstate by Ken Tyler, the printmaker with whom he had previously worked on lithographs for Gemini in Los Angeles. Hockney hadn't intended to delay his journey, but Tyler persuaded him to experiment with a new technique of 'paper pulp', which involved pouring molten coloured-paper pulp into compartmentalised metal moulds, and then transferring the design into a hydraulic press. Unlike a typical print, the 'paper pulp' is a one-off: the image inheres in the actual fabric of the paper. Tyler showed him examples of the process by Ellsworth Kelly and Kenneth Noland, and Hockney was instantly enthralled.

Hockney worked at Ken Tyler's studio for forty-five days to create his memorable series of twenty-nine *Paper Pools*, vibrant colouristic evocations of Tyler's swimming pool, in which a yellow diving board hovers over luminous water. Tyler later described it as 'slave labour … all of us just loved it'. Hockney's mural-style pictures, assembled from grids of six or twelve panels, anticipated the multipanelled format of many later works. Their blocked-out, saturated hues set the tone, moreover, for many of his paintings of the 1980s, in which bold colourism would supersede crisp naturalism.

It wasn't until October that Hockney reached Los Angeles. Almost as soon as he arrived, he had to spend a week in San Francisco – honouring a promise to teach at the Art Institute. Here, he realised that his deafness was worse than ever: he could barely hear some of the students. In Hollywood, a specialist informed him that he had lost a quarter of his hearing and would lose more. 'I will get the hearing aid next week and wear it,' he wrote to Kitaj. 'I shall just have to readjust my persona as a slightly deaf person and paint the hearing aid red and blue.'

Los Angeles in the late 1970s was thriving; its iconic Hollywood sign had just been restored, and Hockney was enchanted by the roller skaters on Hollywood Boulevard, sensing that if Brueghel came to LA, this would be what he would paint. He had rented a house on Miller Drive, above Sunset Boulevard, not far from the Chateau Marmont. Maurice Payne, his new assistant and an expert in print-making, had organised a studio in a former furniture store on Santa Monica Boulevard. Hockney embarked on a twenty-foot-wide scene of the street outside. The frieze-like panorama *Santa Monica Boulevard* was based on shots taken with his Pentax camera, and employed a new kind of luminous acrylic paint used in animation: as shoppers stroll on the sidewalk, men strut and loiter. Hockney loved the district's hustlers and the way they looked like ordinary hitchhikers. While making the painting, he invited men off the street to comment on the work-in-progress.

Soon afterwards, Hockney learned of plans for an exhibition of his works on paper by an aspiring dealer called Peter Goulds, a Londoner who had first come to California in 1972 to lecture at UCLA's Video Workshop before founding the L.A. Louver gallery (named after the slatted, manoeuvrable windows popular in the city) on North Venice Boulevard in 1975. Goulds had managed to purchase or borrow a copy of every print Hockney had made. Hockney met with him and agreed to contribute a group of new line drawings to the show. *Drawings and Prints: 1961–1977*, which opened on a Sunday afternoon in November 1978, announced the artist's return to LA – and marked the inception of a forty-year working relationship. All the expensive prints in the show sold immediately, leaving a number of cheaper works that took years to shift. Goulds recounted in an interview in 2011: 'At the end David came up to me and did something no man had ever done to me. He kissed me right on the lips. Then just said, "Thank you so much, love" and off he went.'

One morning in February 1979, Hockney received a phone call from his brother, telling him that their father had died from a heart attack. He was in New York when he received the news, on his way back to California, having only recently been in England with his family (his parents had come down to London for a showing of the *Paper Pools*, staying at the Savoy). He returned at once. Kenneth Hockney had wanted his body to be donated to Leeds University for research, but this wish couldn't be honoured because there had been an autopsy. Instead, he was cremated. The family made a printed card for the funeral decorated with coloured spots, recalling the way in which Kenneth used to put fluorescent spots on his letters to attract attention to something he wanted to emphasise.

From his apartment on Miller Drive, Hockney moved in the summer of 1979 into a rented house on Montcalm Avenue in the Hollywood Hills, one of a cluster of wooden bungalow-style properties on a tucked-away road. Built in the late 1940s and featuring a dramatic double-height living area, the property had been found for him by Gregory Evans, whom Hockney had persuaded to come to Los Angeles as a live-in assistant. In the living room, Hockney hung a painting by his father of Laurel and Hardy. Beyond the sliding doors was a wooden terrace overlooking a swimming pool. The entire plot was encompassed by palm trees. The pool became a favourite motif in his work, although different now from in the earlier paintings, in that he concentrated more minutely on the plays of light on the water's surface.

That summer, Peter Schlesinger was back in California visiting his parents. Hockney painted his former lover for the final time, in a picture that shows him sitting at a table, reaching for a bottle and glass. Hockney has held onto the painting, never allowing it to be exhibited or reproduced. He also drew and painted Divine, the larger-than-life star of John Waters's cult films, whom he had met (at Divine's request) through Don Bachardy. He made two paintings of the drag icon, one of which remained unfinished. The other was bought, somewhat incongruously, by Richard Mellon

Scaife, an ardent supporter of conservative causes; it was later gifted to the Carnegie Institute.

Two years previously, Hockney had been invited to design a new production at the Metropolitan Opera in New York: a triple bill of French works comprising Erik Satie's ballet *Parade*, and the two operas *Les Mamelles de Tirésias* by Poulenc and *L'Enfant et les sortilèges* by Ravel, scheduled for 1981. Rudolf Nureyev was brought in to choreograph *Parade*, although he squabbled with the director, John Dexter, and Hockney, with Dexter writing in his diary: 'The problem is to prevent the Russian cuckoo throwing the English golden eggs out of the nest!' In the end, the Russian cuckoo was sacked from the project.

Back in London for the summer of 1980, Hockney worked intensively on the designs, along with sixteen paintings and drawings on related themes of dance and music. In the autumn, invigorated by his work for the Metropolitan Opera, he re-embraced Los Angeles – and its heightened colours – as a subject. *Santa Monica Boulevard*, despite its dazzling hues, had been too much aligned with the naturalism and frontality of earlier compositions – asphyxiated, as he saw it, by supposedly 'real' perspective. Now, he conjured the terrain and architecture of the city in works that dispensed with traditional perspective, multiplying the points of view. Driving every day from the Hollywood Hills down to Santa Monica Boulevard and back, he gained a new impression of Los Angeles; in the past it had solely been a city of straight lines and cubes. The winding topography of the hills was translated into his pictures, where previously the only wiggly lines had been those dancing on the surface of water.

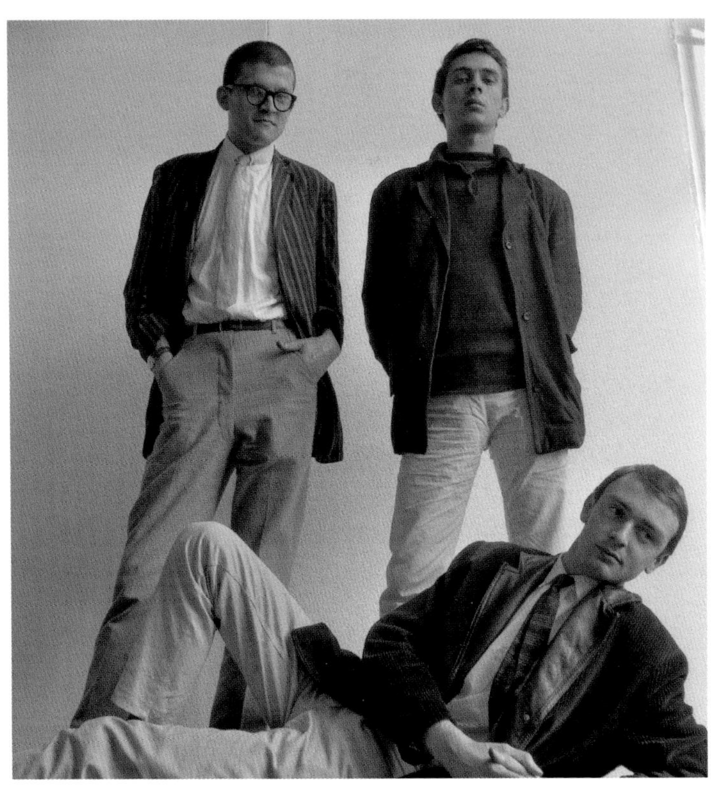

David Hockney, Peter Phillips and
Peter Crutch, Royal College of Art, London, 1961

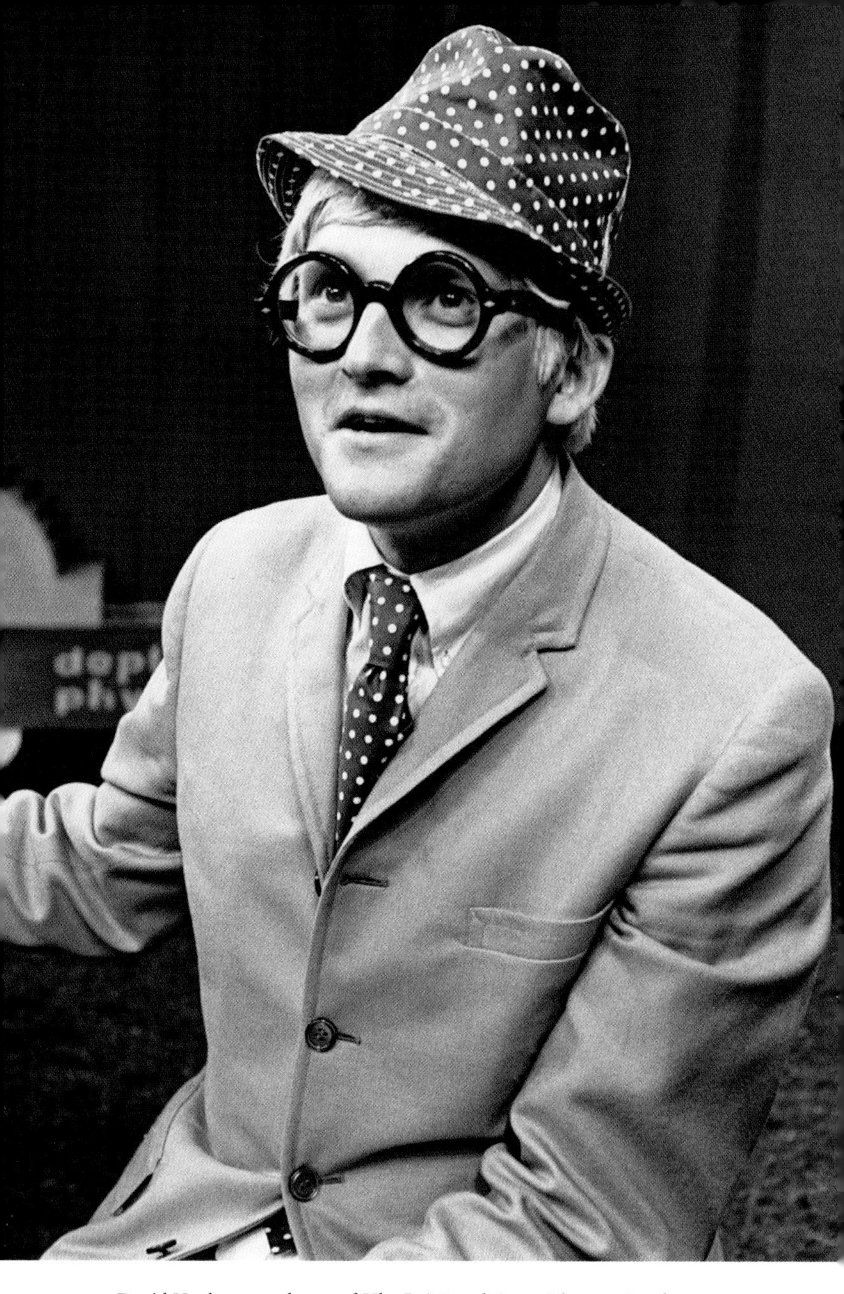

David Hockney on the set of *Ubu Roi*, Royal Court Theatre, London, 1966

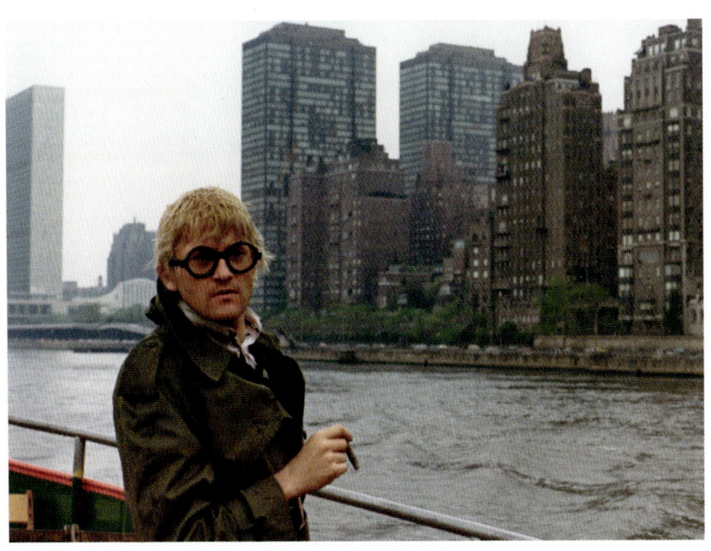

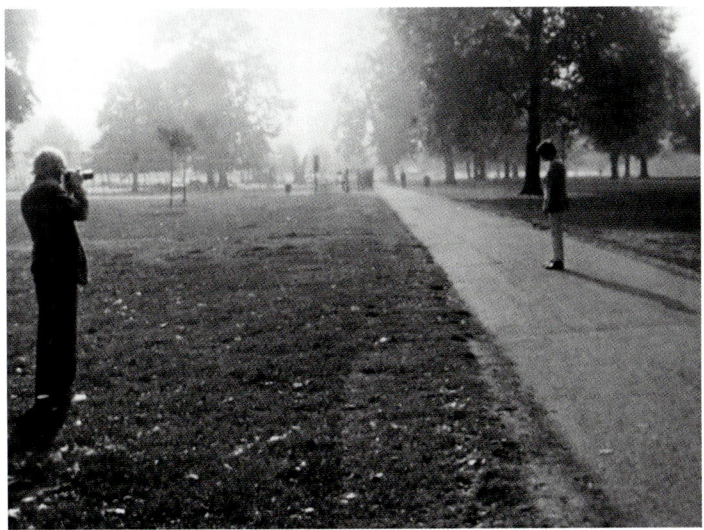

TOP – David Hockney, New York, 1972,
in footage by Jack Hazan for *A Bigger Splash* (1974)

ABOVE – David Hockney and Peter Schlesinger,
Kensington Gardens, London, 1972

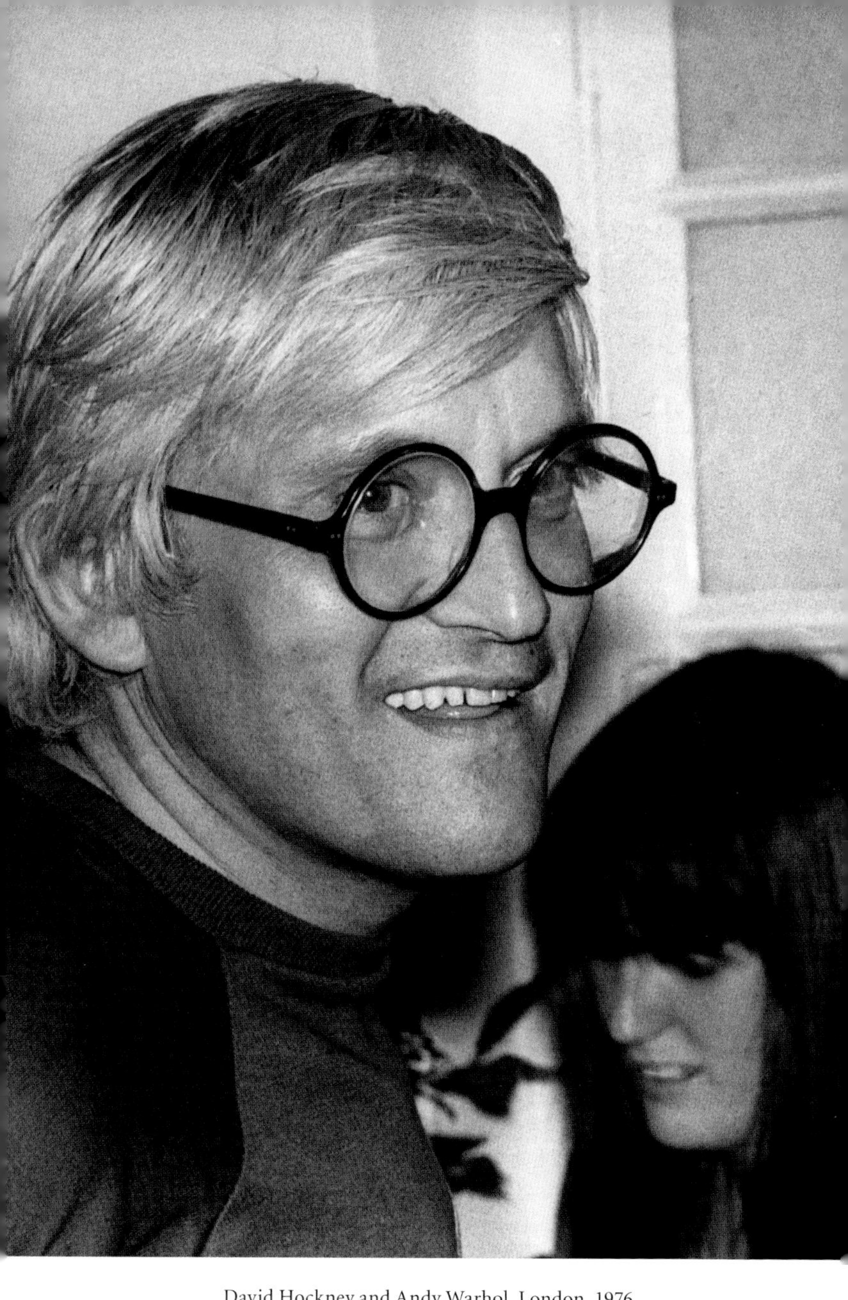

David Hockney and Andy Warhol, London, 1976

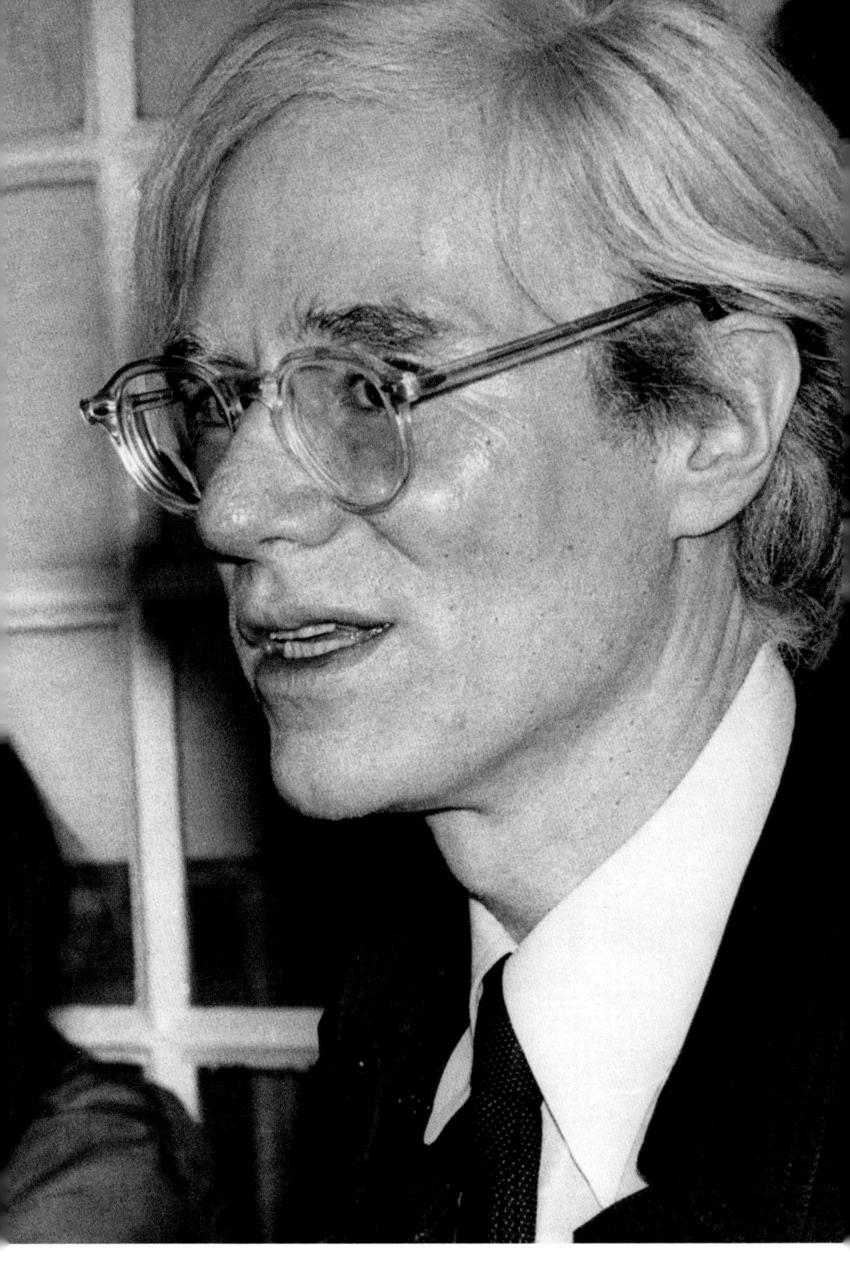

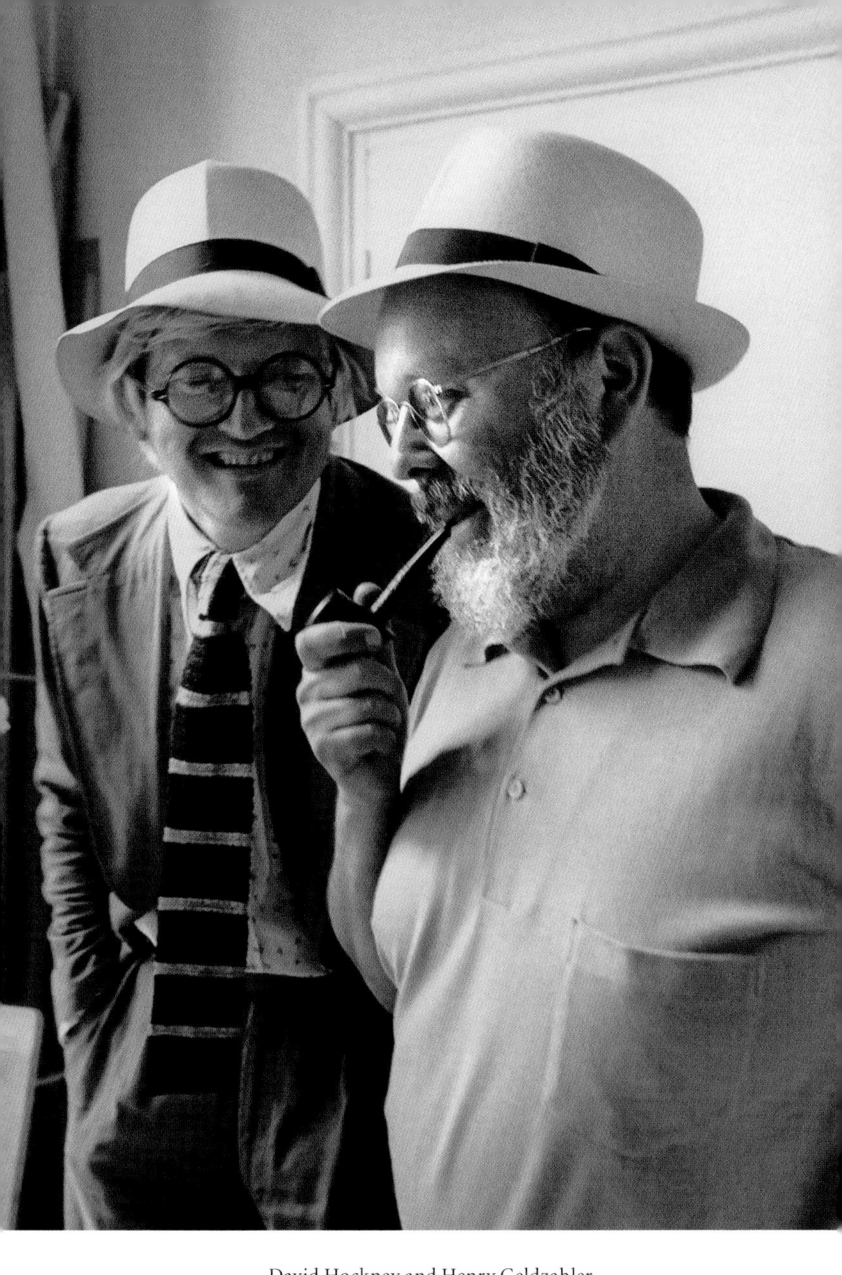

David Hockney and Henry Geldzahler
on Hockney's thirty-eighth birthday, Paris, 1975

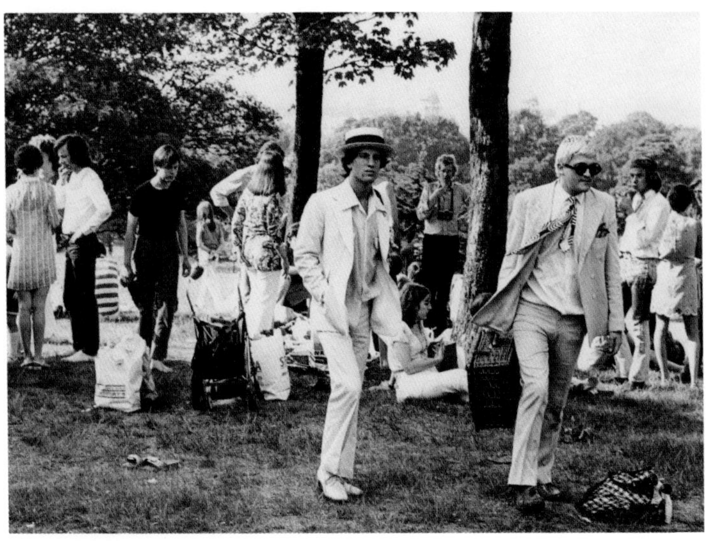

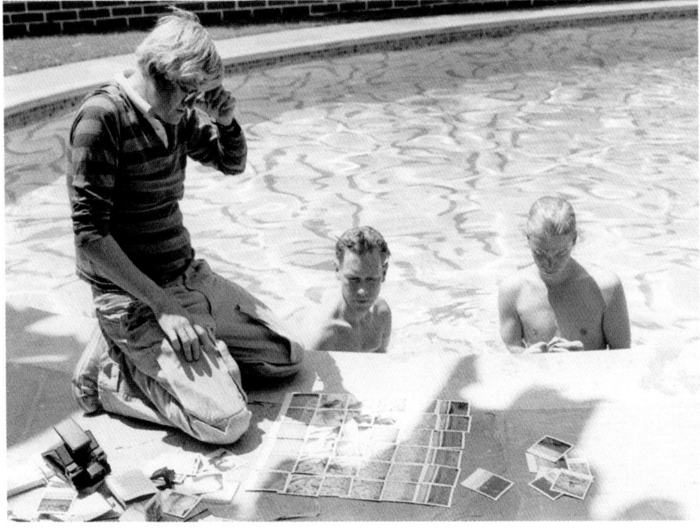

top – Peter Schlesinger and David Hockney,
Greenwich Park, London, 1969

above – David Hockney, David Stoltz and Ian Falconer,
Montcalm Avenue, Los Angeles, 1982

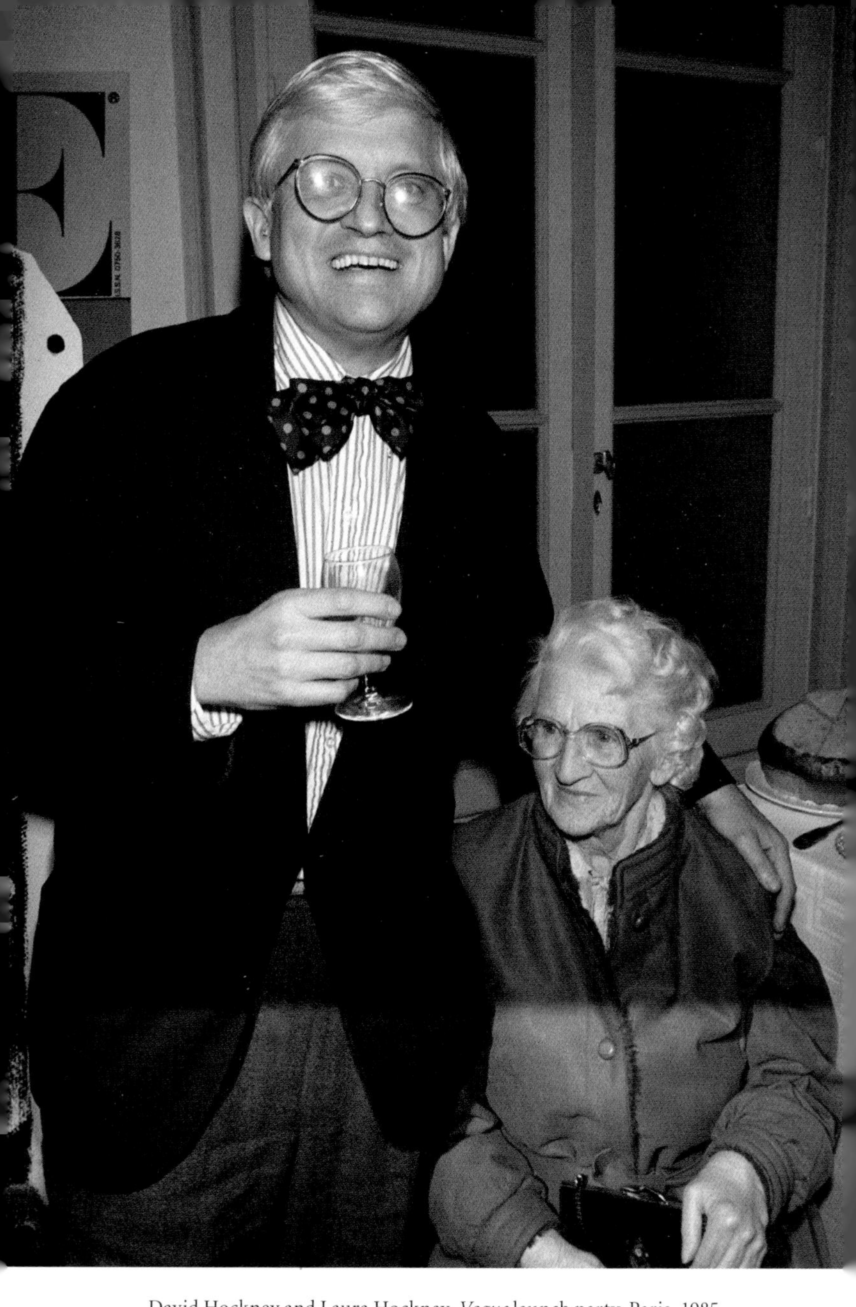

David Hockney and Laura Hockney, *Vogue* launch party, Paris, 1985

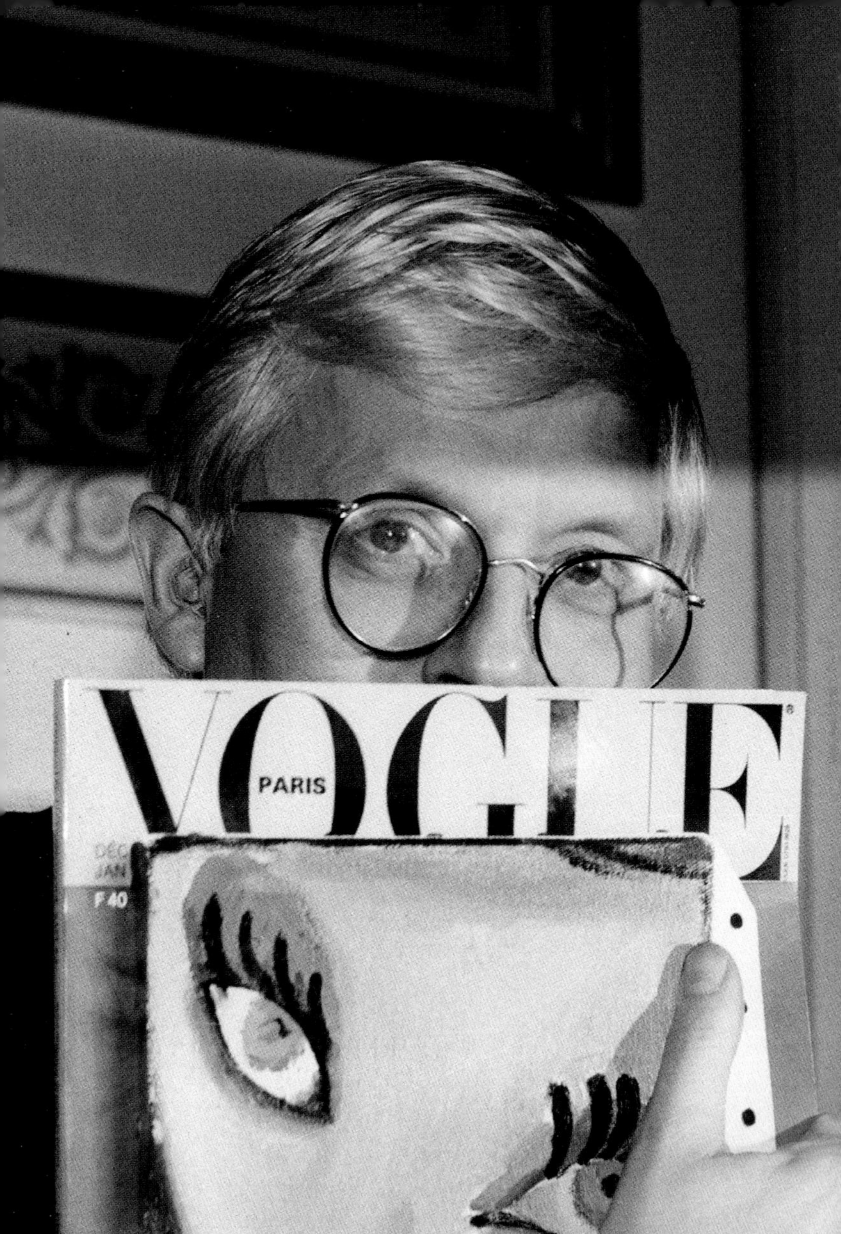
VOGUE
PARIS
DÉC
JAN
F 40

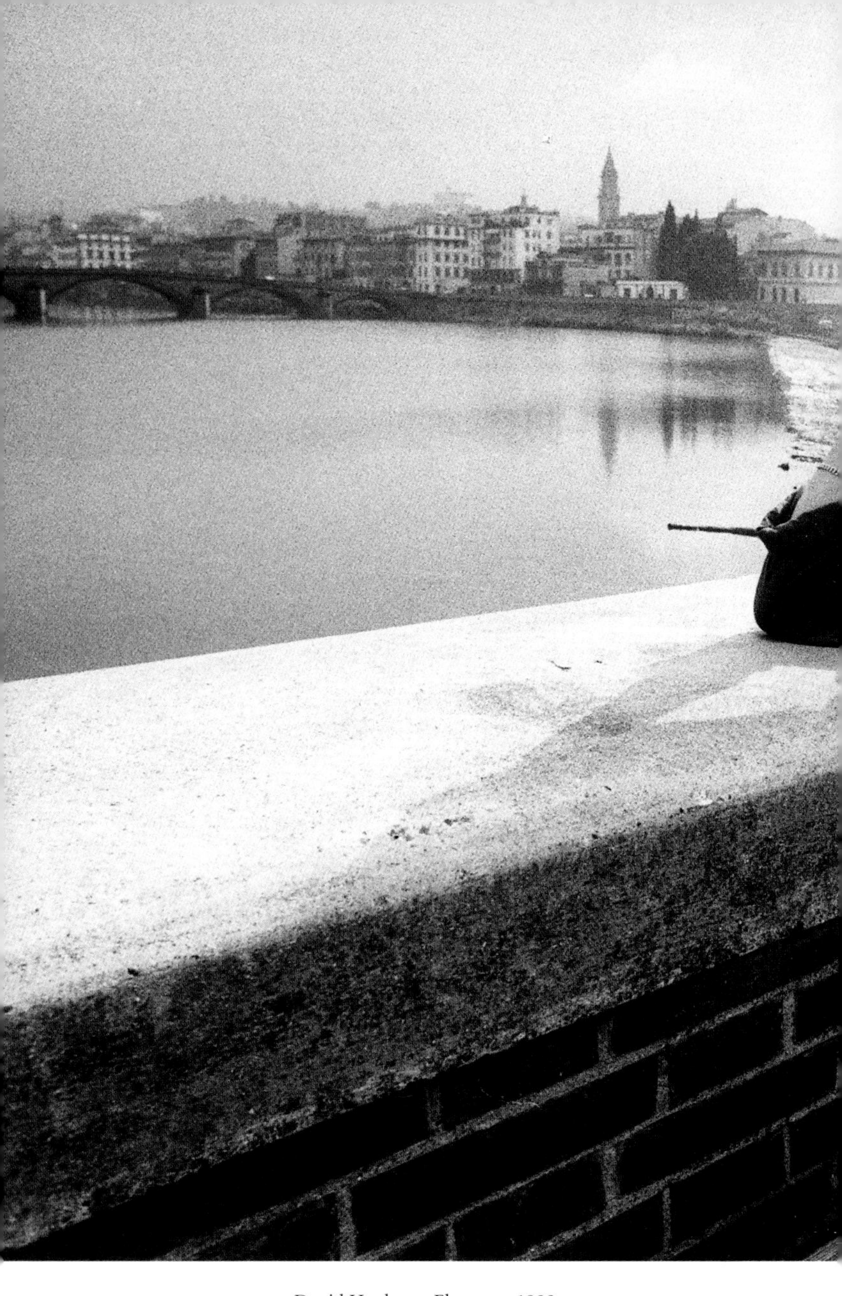

David Hockney, Florence, 1988

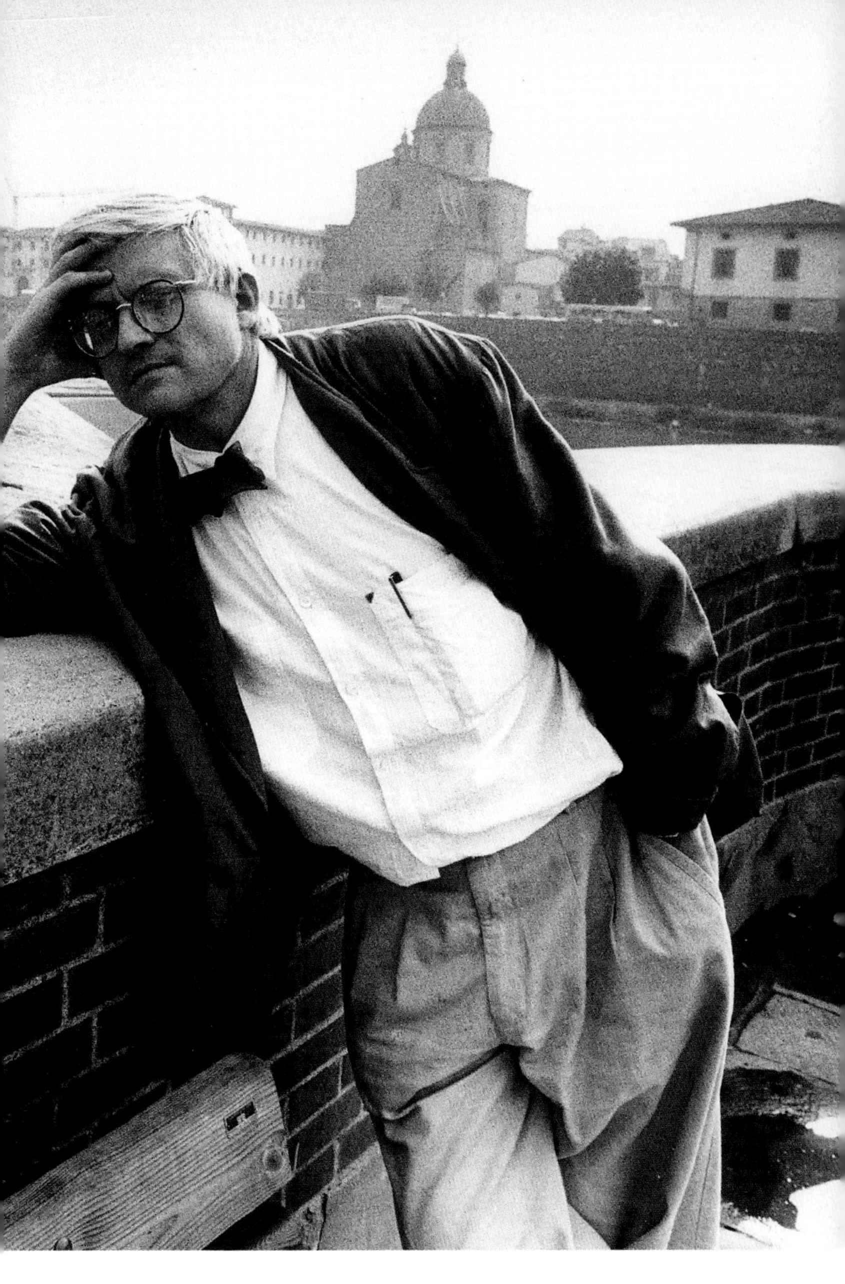

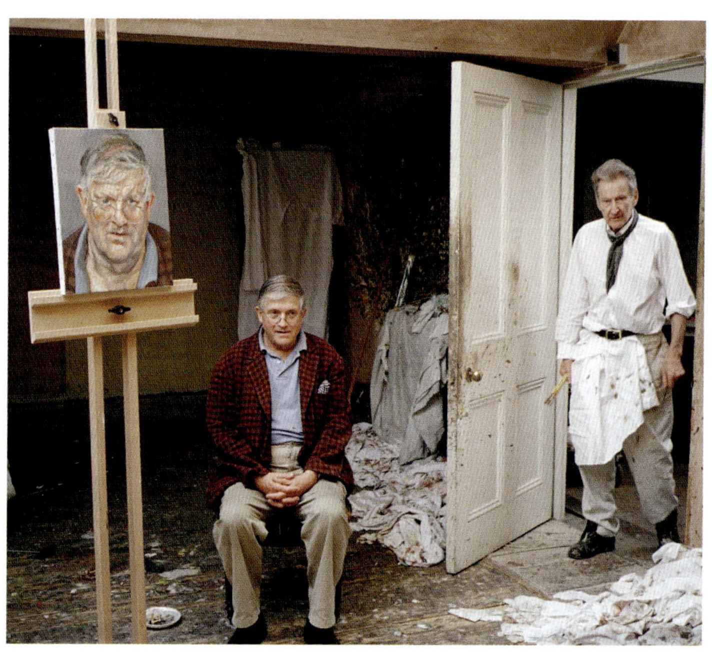

David Hockney and Lucian Freud, London, 2002

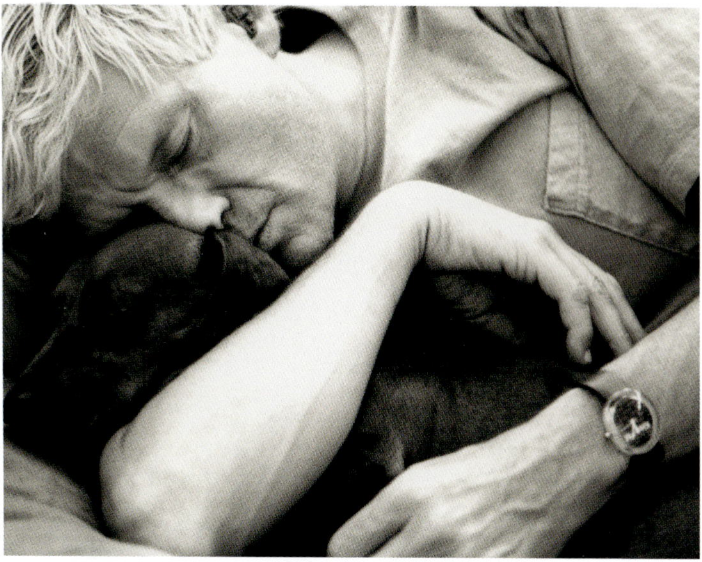

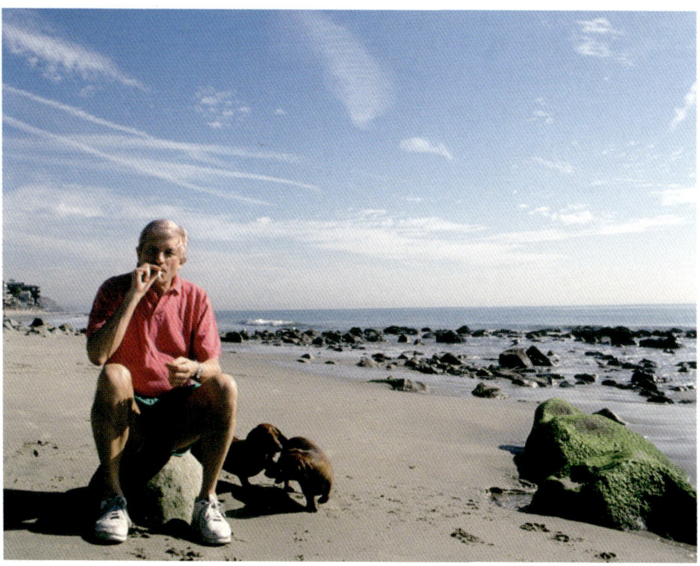

TOP – David Hockney and dachshund, 1993

ABOVE – David Hockney with Stanley and Boodgie, Malibu, 1994

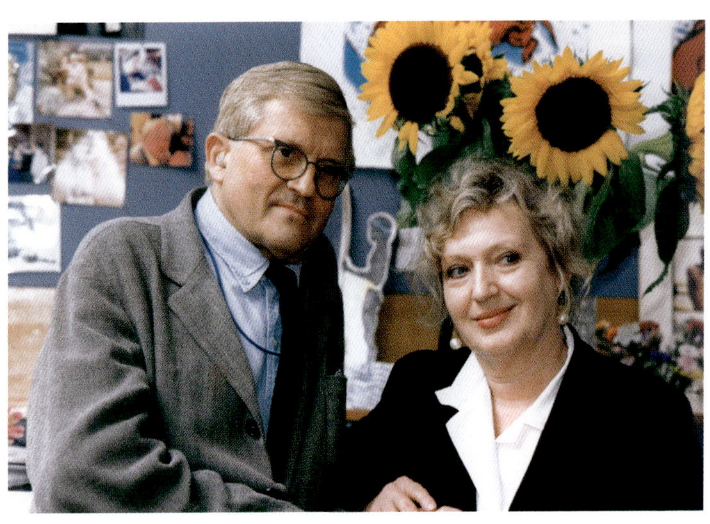

David Hockney and Celia Birtwell, 1996

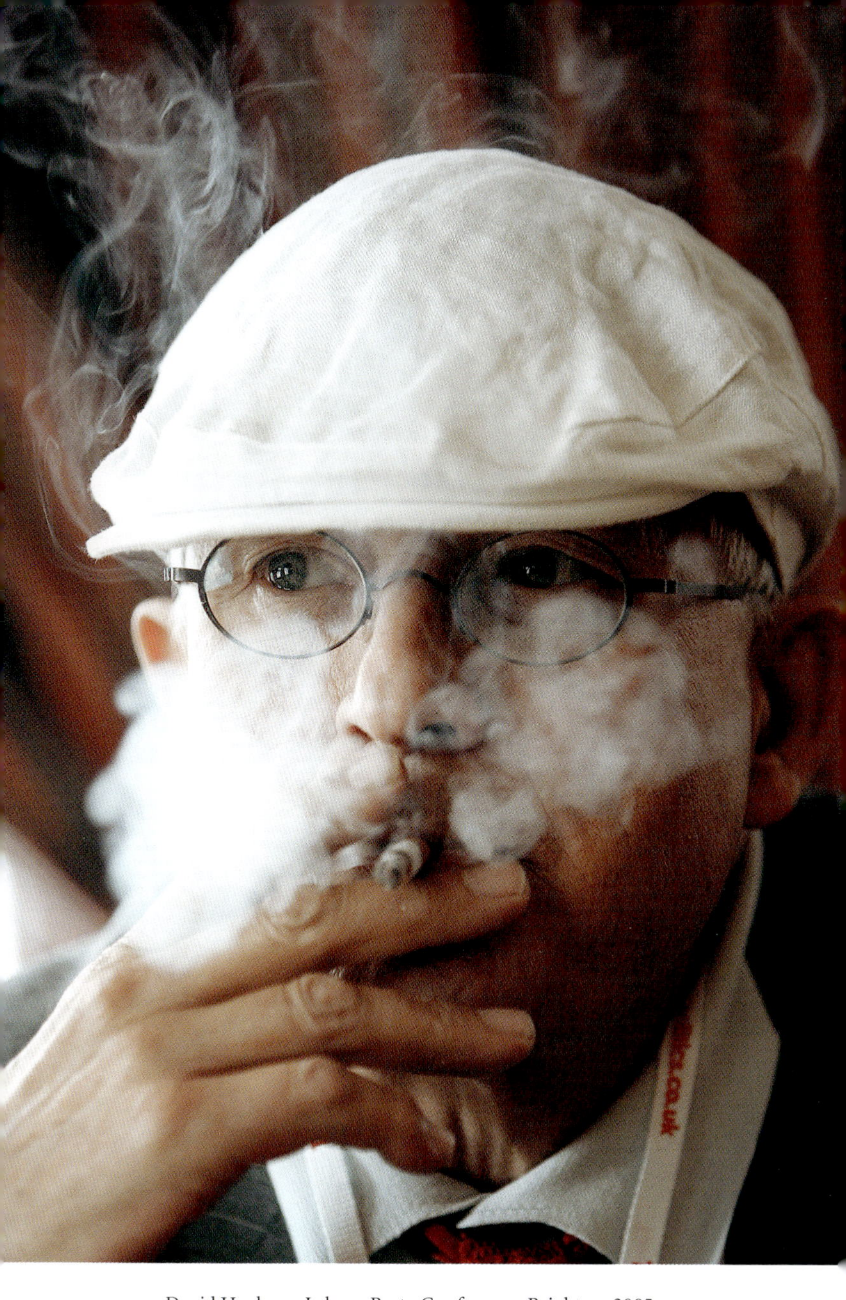

David Hockney, Labour Party Conference, Brighton, 2005

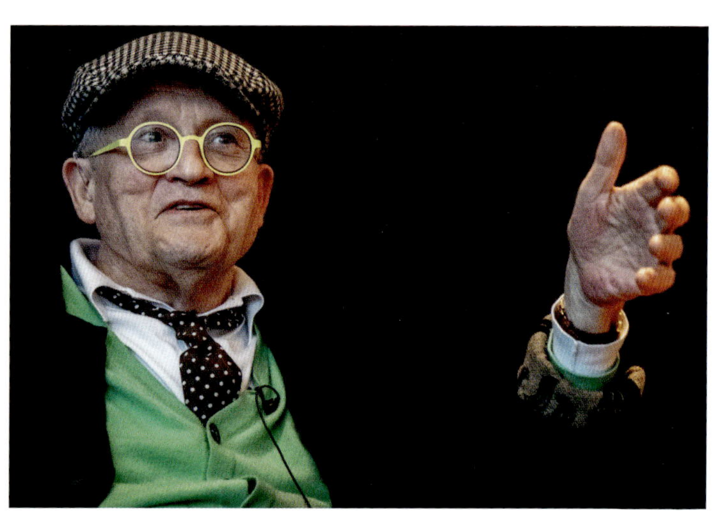

David Hockney, 2019

The watercolour *Nichols Canyon Road and Hollywood Boulevard* gave rise to a seven-by-five-foot painting, *Nichols Canyon*, completed in late 1980. Painted from memory, it evokes the freedom and allure of driving through the hills: the image of a shaded road winding through sunlit plots of tilting land recalls Christopher Isherwood's description of the same landscape in his novel *A Single Man* (1964): 'And how charming it is! An up-and-down terrain of steep little hills with white houses of cracked stucco perched insecurely on their sides and tops.' Developing the theme, Hockney began work on a new seven-by-twenty-foot canvas, which would become *Mulholland Drive: The Road to the Studio*.

# 7.

# A New Spirit: From California to Tokyo, 1981–88

For three weeks, Hockney worked continuously on his giant painting of Mulholland Drive. The road of the title cuts a meandering course across the painting, with the Hollywood Hills spreading beneath it in bursts of lilac, green and blue. Above, to the north, the San Fernando Valley appears as a map-like grid.

The work was shown together with *Experimental Canyon Painting* (1978), *Nichols Canyon* (1980) and *Divine* (1979) in the exhibition *A New Spirit in Painting* at the Royal Academy, London, in January 1981. This was a broad anthology of three generations of painters, and a groundbreaking restatement of the medium's power and plurality after the ascendancy of minimalist and conceptual art. And yet the show was controversial even before it opened, with the academicians at war over its merits. One of the curators, Norman Rosenthal, recalled later that it was the progressives – rather than the conservatives – who objected, perceiving something retrograde in the exhibition's premise. Spurred on by a whispering campaign, Hockney and Kitaj turned up during the hanging to demand the removal of their works. The critic David Sylvester, who happened to be present, managed to talk them out of it.

Hockney's new paintings prompted mixed reactions. Marina Vaizey, writing in *The Sunday Times*, referred to them as 'demented needlework'. But if the critics of the London show were equivocal, the premiere of the *Parade* triple bill in New York in February drew rave reviews. *The New York Times* described the sets as a 'fluorescent thread' running through the production. By this time, Hockney was already working on his next project for the Met. The previous November, director John Dexter had invited him to work on yet another triple bill, this time a trio of works by Igor Stravinsky, *Le Sacre du printemps*, *Le Rossignol* and *Oedipus Rex*, scheduled for December 1981.

At home in Bradford for Christmas, Hockney painted the interior of his rented house on Montcalm Avenue from memory. A trip to China earlier in the year had strengthened his inclination to work from imagination rather than observation. Across three canvases, the living room and terrace beyond are evoked through slanting planes of colour, not unlike the sets he had worked on that year. Hockney was in a position to buy the house outright the following year (from the actor couple Tony Perkins and Berry Berenson). In celebration, he emptied the pool and painted the insides a luminous shade of azure, overspread by darker blue arcs ('Dufyesque' marks, trailing drips). Inscribed in the centre of the pool was 'D.H. 82'. The insides of the house were decorated in brilliant shades of green, red, blue and yellow inspired by his work on *Parade*. Over the following year, the property transformed into a 'set for living', filled with objects including a set of wooden pigs made by Mo McDermott and his wife, Lisa Lombardi, and – in the artist's bedroom – a painting by Picasso (*Artist and Model*, 1965).

Another addition to the household was Ian Falconer, a twenty-two-year-old designer whom Hockney had met in New York. Falconer was originally a friend of Henry Geldzahler's; the artist met him at a party and invited him to watch a rehearsal of *Parade*, after which they came to see more and more of one another. By late 1981, Hockney had persuaded him to enrol at the Otis Art College in LA, and to move into Montcalm Avenue.

Their romantic involvement was reflected in a number of sensuous drawings of Falconer, including charcoal sketches of the pair making love (preparation for a painting that never came about) and a group of six drawings called *Waking Up*. One of these comically reimagines Hockney waking up and touching Falconer, a habit which the latter (possibly sleeping off a hangover) didn't like – he would poke Hockney back. 'He thought [my body] was beautiful, but I didn't, so it never really quite worked,' Falconer has remarked. 'And I liked to sleep late and he was always pestering me in the morning.' The pair lived upstairs, while Evans, whose day-to-day occupation was the running of the house, occupied a bedroom downstairs. The new situation was challenging for Evans: despite the casualness of his own relationship with Hockney, he felt displaced – and began to lean more heavily on alcohol and drugs. Hockney's response was to bury himself in work and turn a blind eye. 'I wasn't the only person in the house on drugs,' Evans later admitted, 'but it was a problem I had to deal with'. At the encouragement of Mo McDermott and Lisa Lombardi, he went to a clinic and got clean.

The pool at Montcalm Avenue – the turquoise calm at the centre of the emotional storm – features prominently in the Polaroids that Hockney began to take that year, prompted in part by a proposal from the Centre Georges Pompidou for an exhibition of his photographic work. He had long been sceptical about the merits of the medium, sardonically observing that photography 'is all right if you don't mind looking at the world from the point of view of a paralyzed Cyclops – *for a split second*'. He relayed this view to Alain Sayag, a curator from the Pompidou, who had come to stay for four days to look through his many photograph albums. Each night, Hockney and Sayag argued about whether photography is a good medium for an artist.

Once Sayag had made his selection from Hockney's albums, a problem came to light: the negatives for the prints were jumbled together in boxes, and it would take too long to sort them and make copies before Sayag had to leave. And so he and Hockney went to a local store and bought several boxes of Polaroid SX-70 film, which they used to make instant photographs of the prints that Sayag had chosen. Afterwards, Hockney was left with stacks of unused film.

The next day, he found a solution to the problem of photography's fixed viewpoint by assembling numerous Polaroids taken of the same subject – from multiple angles – into a grid. The first experiment consisted of thirty Polaroids of his house, repeating the inside–outside movement of his recent paintings (interior, deck, pool). The house appeared as a disjointed amalgam, crisscrossed by the white borders of the Polaroids. The result struck him as a close approximation of the experience of seeing, and an echo of the fractured and juddering imagery of Cubist painting, whereby different views are synthesised into an unstable whole.

The thirty-part view of the house was the first of the 'Polaroid joiners', as Hockney came to describe them. He was exhilarated by the new format, and would make 140 joiners between February and May of 1982. People became his preferred subject. Isherwood and Bachardy were captured on 6 March, seated and standing in matching linen suits (Isherwood told Hockney that he was behaving like a mad scientist with his camera). Nathan Kolodner, a dealer from the Emmerich Gallery, was photographed swimming in the pool. A larger grid of 120 Polaroids shows Evans swimming, his pale body fractured and multiplied across the individual photographs, streaking through the blocks of turquoise water. Hockney likened the effect to that of a ceiling painting by Tiepolo. The photographer Bill Brandt and his wife, Noya, were shown staring down in fascination at the incomplete grid of photographs Hockney was creating (each Polaroid took around a minute to process, and so the assembly of a work was slow, requiring a prolonged sitting).

A selection of the joiners was shown at the Emmerich Gallery in June under the title *Drawing with a Camera*. The following month, the Pompidou opened its comprehensive survey of Hockney's photographs, combining private snapshots with his more recent experiments. In September, he evolved the composite technique further by using his

Pentax 110 – rather than a Polaroid camera – to capture scenery in California, Utah and Arizona, including the Grand Canyon. When the prints had been processed, he assembled them into expansive photo-collages, sprawling syntheses of individual prints out of which a panoramic view, witnessed from changing angles, is reconstructed. Often, the tips of Hockney's feet are visible at the base of the image.

Over the following nine months, travelling through London, Bradford, New York, Minneapolis and Japan, Hockney made some 200 photo-collages. While in Yorkshire in November, he photographed his mother in the grounds of the ruined Bolton Abbey. She is seen seated on the edge of a gravestone, wrapped from head to foot in a green raincoat. The abbey was one of the places where Laura and Kenneth had courted half a century earlier.

Hockney continued to take photographs for collages during a trip to Tokyo in February 1983 with Evans. He had travelled to Tokyo to speak at a conference, along with Robert Rauschenberg, about the uses of paper in art. At the end of the lunch, over coffee, he spent twenty-five minutes capturing everything around him using his Pentax. *Luncheon at the British Embassy, Tokyo* amalgamates the photographic prints into a scattered mass, all taken from the single vantage point of Hockney's chair (his place card is visible at the bottom of the fragmentary assemblage). The panelled interior and conversing embassy officials and their wives – observed in dozens of photographic 'glances' – have faded, over time, to a uniform shade of pinkish-brown. Other sites he treated using the same technique were the rock garden at the Ryōanji Temple in Kyoto, centred on a sea of pebbles, and Evans, captured in intimate studies that perhaps carry a note of elegy for their love affair.

An equally personal image was that of Joe MacDonald, captured in the spring of 1983 in his New York apartment. Hockney had seen a lot of him since 1979, while working in New York on the *Parade* designs, and they had often sampled the city's gay clubs and bathhouses together. Shortly after the premiere of the Stravinsky triple bill in December 1981, MacDonald fell ill with what would turn out to be AIDS. Hockney brought him to Los Angeles for a while to recuperate, but could see that his friend was very unwell. The collage shows MacDonald standing in the doorway of his New York living room, flanked by works by Hockney. He died a few weeks later, the first of the artist's friends to be killed by the disease, and the first prominent figure in the fashion world.

That same year, Hockney sanctioned the production of editions of forty-two of his photo-collages. Ten assistants worked at his studio on Santa Monica Boulevard under the supervision of David Graves to create multiple replicas of each composition, using reprints of the constituent photographs. The resulting editions were exhibited in the summer of 1983 at galleries around the world. He was elated to receive a letter from the great French photographer Henri Cartier-Bresson telling him how wonderful the works were. Despite the creation of a frenetic production line, Hockney was nonchalant about their market value. He had a stamp made for the editions that read: 'Not for investment. Buy only for pleasure.'

As much as a riposte to the art market, the collages were a fresh expression of Hockney's creative range and ambition. His breadth of output was again underlined in November, when he opened a major exhibition at the Walker Art Center, Minneapolis, devoted to his stage designs. This featured full-scale tableaux based on his various theatrical sets, alongside original models and related paintings. Following its run in Minneapolis, the show toured around North America and Europe for two years. At the end of 1983, Hockney went to London for an exhibition of his photographic work at the Hayward Gallery.

Amid this volume and variety of activity, life at Montcalm Avenue remained riven with tensions. Animosity had developed between Gregory Evans and Ian Falconer. By the autumn of 1983, Falconer had had enough and decided to move out. Evans became mired once more in heavy drinking. Observing the goings-on, Henry Geldzahler wryly nicknamed the house 'Mont Hysterical'.

In 1984, after a break of almost four years, Hockney returned to painting. He used the term 'New Cubism' to describe his paintings of the mid-1980s, a mode that drew inspiration not only from the synchronous perspectives of Picasso, but Einstein's theory of relativity and the teachings of the Chinese philosopher Lao-Tze. An interviewer visiting him at the Mayflower Hotel in New York in 1984 observed books on the latter two subjects piled on the coffee table.

Hockney's first major painting following his long photographic phase, bearing witness to his ongoing fascination with Cubism, was *A Visit with Mo and Lisa, Echo Park,*

*Los Angeles* (1984), a gouache based on the Echo Park home of Mo McDermott and his wife. The couple had moved to their new house after a stint in rehab, and seemed to have turned their lives around. In Hockney's scene, outside and inside space – landscape , interiors, sky – unfold in the style of a Chinese scroll painting in which every feature is seen in close-up as the eye travels through the picture.

At the same time, Hockney began *A Visit with Christopher and Don, Santa Monica Canyon*, a two-canvas work measuring six feet high and twenty feet wide. Based on gouache sketches made in situ at the house of his friends, this panoramic composition was conceived as a playing out of nonlinear narratives. Again, Hockney drew influence from Chinese landscape scrolls in which the scene unrolls into view. (He had studied examples at the Metropolitan Museum in New York; and one Sunday in 1986, he would spend hours poring over a seventy-foot scroll shown to him by the curator of Chinese art, an experience he recalled as one of the most memorable days of his life.) At the top of the picture is the streaking yellow form of Adelaide Drive, Santa Monica. The painting then provides fractured visions of the house – living room, terrace, bedroom, steps outside – and beyond to the beach, sea and sky. Isherwood and Bachardy appear as faint linear presences, almost invisible within the hectic design. Isherwood was ill, by this point, with prostate cancer. Hockney had noticed the way he clenched his hands frequently.

That summer, Hockney travelled to Mexico with Evans and David Graves, where he made a series of drawings of a hotel courtyard in Acatlán. The following February, he and Evans holidayed on the Caribbean island of Mustique, which was notorious by that time as a hangout of the rich and bohemian, with Princess Margaret among the island's long-term habitués. Here, they were joined by Nathan Kolodner from the Emmerich Gallery. Hockney was invited to join the Mustique cricket match, a yearly event organised by the photographer Lord Lichfield – neighbour and cousin to Princess Margaret – in which the high-society English visitors played the Caribbean locals.

In July 1985, Hockney went to Arles in the south of France to deliver a lecture on photography at the Rencontres de la Photographie, an annual festival that had been held in the town since 1970. There, he was approached by Paul Wagner, the art director of French *Vogue*, who invited him to contribute a forty-two-page feature to the magazine. Hockney agreed, on condition that he be allowed complete editorial control. Back in his LA studio, he pinned up forty-two blank sheets of paper on the wall. The resulting feature, published in December, was a wide-ranging, freeform compilation of drawings, photographs and handwritten text. The magazine's cover featured a portrait of Celia Birtwell in the style of one of Picasso's muses.

Building upon the arguments of his lecture in Arles, Hockney's *Vogue* essay included detailed annotations on the significance of reverse perspective and the alienating effects of the one-point perspective of the High Renaissance. The feature included photo-collages of the Luxembourg Gardens and the Place de Furstenberg, together with other glimpses – variously staged and spontaneous – of the artist's life. One is a view over a car steering wheel described as *une scène typique Hollywoodienne.* Through the windscreen, on a sunny mountain road, a man in tiny shorts thumbs a lift. The Hollywood sign is just visible on the horizon. Encapsulating Hockney's lifelong pacifism, the last words of the *Vogue* feature were *Paix sur terre* – peace on earth.

Hockney attended a gala dinner at the White House in late 1985, the guest of President Ronald Reagan and his wife, Nancy, where he caused some consternation by turning up on foot. Other guests included the Prince and Princess of Wales: this was the famed occasion on which Princess Diana danced with John Travolta (her off-the-shoulder evening gown has gone down in history as the 'Travolta dress'). Hockney was on the President's table, along with Diana. When he rose to speak, Reagan became confused, making a toast to 'Prince Charles and Princess David'.

In late 1985, Hockney's close relationship with Gregory Evans came to an end. Evans's drug and alcohol use had finally driven a wedge between them. After another treatment programme, Evans decided that he had to spend time away from Montcalm Avenue. For the next five years, during which time he set up a teapot and fabric shop, they were barely in contact.

A parallel and progressive loss suffered by Hockney was that of his hearing. In 1985, he wrote to his old friend Kitaj:

… over the last years, to compensate for my muffled ears, I've been developing a strong visual space sense. I say this because I'm very aware that I seem to see in another way that has to do with noticing movement of the eye (time) and perception of space. A blind man

develops his hearing to define his space; could not
a deaf man develop his sight? ... Anyway, there's no
doubt that either from the theatre or somewhere else,
I've been becoming more aware of time and space.

Hockney made very few paintings at this time. Instead,
modern technology was proving an irresistible draw. In
December, he was invited by BBC producer Michael Deakin
to try out a new computerised tool called the Quantel
Paintbox. This had been developed four years earlier for
television graphics. The experiment was recorded in one
of a series of programmes, *Painting with Light.* For eight
hours, Hockney used an electronic pen to work on a plain
surface, drawing images directly onto a television monitor.
His doodlings on the Quantel Paintbox, which included
an attempt to draw Francis Bacon from memory, were
forerunners of his iPad and iPhone drawings of more recent
years. The rendering of Bacon – first in turquoise, then a
more accurate shade of pink – grew into a florid mess which
Hockney 'painted' over with a portrait of David Graves.

Not long after, Hockney transferred his attentions to the
colour photocopier, discovering in this mundane utility an
unlikely printing device. By feeding the same sheets through
the machine multiple times, he found that he could create
subtle gradations of colour. He called the results 'Home
Made Prints'. The photocopier would occupy him for a
seven-month stretch.

The following April, *Vanity Fair* asked Hockney
if he would create illustrations for an article by Gregor
von Rezzori, re-enacting the journey of Vladimir Nabokov's

Humbert Humbert (the narrator of *Lolita*) across the United States. Together with David Graves and Charlie Scheips (a young curator who had come to work for Hockney that month), he set out on a road trip through the Mojave Desert. They drove for three days before finding the right setting, a crossroads on Pearblossom Highway north of Los Angeles. Hockney then spent a further eight days shooting the location, often using a ladder to photograph the road signs in close-up.

The result was a photo-collage titled *Pearblossom Hwy., 11–18th April 1986*. This marked the grand culmination of his four-year exploration of the technique. A cluster of road signs on the right evokes the experience of driving and attending to notices, while the more open view of the Antelope Valley on the left – including litter strewn on the roadside – replicates the wandering gaze of a passenger. *Vanity Fair* decided not to use the image following a disagreement with Hockney over the final presentation. But the project had resulted in the most painterly and beautiful of his photo-collages. He made a second, larger version of *Pearblossom Hwy*. Both works ended up in the Getty Museum.

In October 1986, Hockney began work on the designs for Jonathan Miller's production of Wagner's *Tristan und Isolde* in December 1987 at the Los Angeles Music Center Opera. The project, which he conceived as a series of gargantuan paintings, occupied him for a year. He had a model in his studio which he played around with continually, sometimes smoking a joint as he tried out different light effects. He treated friends, including Billy Wilder and Don Bachardy, to dinner parties featuring live 'performances' with the model.

The house was a hive of activity at this time. Scheips did much of the cooking, although Hockney eventually persuaded him to hire someone to do it for him – a young gay man who became known as 'Mike the Chef'. But a shadow was cast on the conviviality by Hockney's worries about Mo McDermott: with his marriage unravelling, McDermott had begun drinking again. Hockney brought him to live and work at his Montcalm studio, but he struggled to settle in.

Around the time of his fiftieth birthday, Hockney's spirits were transformed by the arrival of his first dachshunds, named Stanley (after Stan Laurel) and Rupert. He had been inspired to get them after Ian Falconer acquired a new puppy, Heinz (named after a beautiful youth Isherwood had loved in Berlin). They immediately began to feature in drawings and paintings. Rupert was replaced, after being run over and killed, by Boodgie. In the years to come, Hockney's dogs would figure increasingly in his paintings, and took centre stage in his life – although their lack of house-training exasperated his friends. Due to his deafness, he was now less willing to go out. He did occasionally attend parties, but the image of a gadding celebrity belied the reality. On a trip to New York, he was persuaded by a friend to go to the Palladium, and even though he only stayed for an hour, photographs of him at the disco circulated for weeks after. 'I was never much of a party boy,' he later commented. 'I didn't mind being seen that way, but I am actually a worker. An artist can approve of hedonism, but he can't be a hedonist himself.' His dogs were a convenient pretext for staying at home.

In February 1988, a retrospective exhibition of Hockney's

work opened at the Los Angeles County Museum of Art (LACMA), travelling subsequently to New York and London. Comprising 250 works, this was the first comprehensive survey of his career for eighteen years. Sixteen thousand people passed through the exhibition in its first week in LA. To mark the London show, he was photographed by Helmut Newton for the cover of the colour supplement of *The Sunday Times*. But the lead-up to the Tate opening was overshadowed by his veiled threat in a letter to *The Sunday Times* to withdraw the show (or large sections of it) in protest against Clause 28, the new legislation against the promotion of homosexuality in British schools. Hockney's general hostility towards English society was evident at the press conference for the Tate show in October 1988, where he professed that he had no intention of ever returning to England: 'Los Angeles sun and English puritanism have made me a voluntary exile.'

Escape could be found in more rarefied quarters. That same year, Hockney had recorded the short film *A Day on the Grand Canal with the Emperor of China (or Surface Is Illusion But So Is Depth)*, directed by Philip Haas. In this, he takes a rhapsodic 'journey' down two Chinese scrolls, musing on their different attitude towards time and space as the camera pans along them. LACMA presented the film in its entirety at the retrospective, after a protracted dispute with Hockney over the possibility of playing a shortened version.

Straight after the opening of the retrospective in LA, Charlie Scheips handed in his notice. For him, the hermetic world of Hockney's house and studio had become isolating and claustrophobic. After he left, Scheips wasn't invited to the openings of either the London or New York instalments of the retrospective – a sign, possibly, of the betrayal felt by Hockney when anyone decided to leave him. A more profound loss was that of Mo McDermott a few months later. Hockney's long-term friend, portrayed in *A Bigger Splash* as a wistful observer and anxious protector of the artist, died from alcoholism in May 1988. Hockney was devastated and resentful, regarding the death as a kind of suicide.

# 8.

# Very New Paintings: Malibu and the Wild West, 1989–97

Hockney had bought a beachfront house in Malibu back in 1986. Perched on a rocky promontory, the 1930s property had previously been owned by an elderly lady who was an amateur artist. She had built a small studio on the hill to the rear of the house, accessed via an electric stairlift. Here, in the smallest studio he ever used, Hockney began to work on paintings of the house and its surroundings. His pictures took on the quality of Fauvist stage sets.

While never a permanent base, Malibu became Hockney's sanctuary. He enjoyed going up and down in the stairlift accompanied by his two dachshunds. The interior of the house, glimpsed in paintings such as *Breakfast at Malibu* (1989), was cluttered and homely, a counterpoint to the slick 'Malibu style'. On his car journeys through the hills, he would play Wagner (music – blasted out on his stereo – was still a pleasure, despite his progressing deafness), leading to him creating a route called the 'Wagner drive', a carefully choreographed conjunction of landscape and music that reaches its crescendo at the mountain summit. Walking on the beach with his dog family, at what he referred to as 'the edge of the Western World', was a new pleasure – and a reprieve from grief.

The AIDS crisis had claimed many of his closest friends: Joe MacDonald, Nathan Kolodner, Larry Stanton, Nick Wilder and others. This slow cumulative tragedy coincided with – and helped to catalyse – Hockney's gradual withdrawal from the frenetic social life he had enjoyed in earlier times. He found New York to be permanently changed through the loss of these people; the city was now bereft of its bohemia. His deafness was also making it harder to go out to restaurants or concerts, inclining him towards solitude and privacy. In the late eighties, he worked on a number of small portraits – made quickly from live sittings – of those friends who remained, a testament to loss as much as survival.

In the summer of 1989, a new friend named John Fitzherbert came out to California. Fitzherbert was an Englishman in his early twenties who had previously worked as a chauffeur and chef for John Dexter of the Metropolitan Opera; Hockney had met him while he and Dexter were planning a revival of *Parade* in London. Fitzherbert had then written to Hockney asking if he could join him as a cook in Los Angeles. When he arrived in the Hollywood Hills, Fitzherbert found himself among the entourage of helpers and acolytes that Hockney had gathered around his home – including Richard Schmidt, who now ran the studio at Montcalm Avenue; Ian Falconer, who still lived close by; and Falconer's actor boyfriend, Butch Kirby. Hockney himself was spending most of his time in Malibu. But gradually, he and Fitzherbert embarked on a relationship that would last for two decades.

For a year, Hockney had been using a fax machine, or what he called a 'telephone for the deaf', to communicate with friends and family. He had bought one for himself and one for his sister, Margaret, who lived in Bridlington and who, like Hockney, was profoundly deaf without the assistance of hearing aids. It wasn't long before he began to fax drawings as well. The Malibu house was the point of origin of many of his faxes, which bore the imprint 'From the Hollywood Sea Picture Supply Co.'

His prolific use of the fax machine returned him to the practice of creating pictures out of grids of smaller units. In October 1989, he participated in the São Paulo Biennial – curated that year by Henry Geldzahler – by sending an entire 'show' by fax, to be assembled page by page in Brazil. His decision to contribute in this manner was partly down to the fact that collectors were reluctant to loan his pieces so soon after his 1988 retrospective, but Hockney also took delight in creating large-scale works of art using a technology that most people employed for the sending of contracts and legal paperwork, and that circumvented the rules of the art market. (In the event, owing to poor phone lines between the US and Brazil, the faxes had to be printed in California and carried to the biennial in suitcases.)

The following month, he faxed 144 sheets of fax paper to a friend in Yorkshire, Jonathan Silver, who had opened a museum in an old textile mill in the village of Saltaire, near Bradford. Named the 1853 Gallery, it was dedicated to Hockney's work, but also became a focus for other local artists: the poet and dramatist Tony Harrison staged plays there. The pages comprised a single work, a giant drawing entitled *Tennis*. Their arrival and gradual assembly on the gallery wall were the occasion of a grand public event: 400 guests were invited, including the artist's close friends and family, and Yorkshire Television provided two film crews, one to capture the event in Bradford, and another to record Hockney despatching the faxes from Los Angeles.

California was witnessing the growth of Silicon Valley in this period. At the invitation of the inventors of Photoshop (who had seen his *Pearblossom Hwy.* collage), Hockney travelled up to a three-day workshop which introduced him to computer drawing software – his only previous experience of such technology had been the Quantel Paintbox in 1985. Photoshop gave him an exciting new perspective on image making. He made drawings on an Apple Macintosh computer using the Oasis program, which he then printed on a Canon printer. The workshop also inspired him to invest in a new model of filmless camera which saved images directly onto floppy disks, and which allowed him to print his own images instead of relying on a local photographic shop.

Using the new equipment, he produced *40 Snaps of my House, August 1990*, a collection of small-scale photographic 'details' from his Montcalm Avenue home: chairs, paintbrushes, rocks in the garden, a dachshund on blue-painted decking. His next series using the camera, *112 L.A. Visitors*, consisted of full-length portraits – shot vertically in stages – of visitors to his house. Each figure posed in front of a painting, staring straight ahead in the style of a mugshot. The printouts were pasted together to create near-lifesize renderings of friends and other chance visitors: a journalist, a plumber, a picture-framer.

Long drives through the mountains had meanwhile inspired a sequence of paintings of the Santa Monica coastline. *Pacific Coast Highway and Santa Monica* (1990) – the painting in front of which Hockney posed his 'L.A. Visitors' – evokes the experience of meandering through illuminated hills, looking down at the vast plain of the Los Angeles basin and bay. This and other compositions looked back to Hockney's Hollywood paintings of a decade earlier. His work in this period powerfully reflects his renewed affinity for California. It was this affinity that contributed to his decision in 1990 to decline the offer of a knighthood. Britain and its ingrained traditions felt faraway and irrelevant. 'I didn't want to be Sir David, frankly,' he admitted. The refusal was discreet – he didn't tell anyone – and it wasn't until *The Sunday Times* publicised the fact in 2003 that people knew.

In late 1990, Hockney began work on designs for a production of Puccini's *Turandot*, to open at the Lyric Opera of Chicago in January 1992. Concurrently, he was working on Strauss's *Die Frau ohne Schatten* ('The Woman without a Shadow'), to be directed by John Cox at Covent Garden in 1992. Ian Falconer designed the costumes for both. It was a time of frenetic and unremitting work, and the strain finally took its toll. One evening in November, Hockney couldn't make it up the stairs to his bedroom. John Fitzherbert drove him to hospital, where he was told he had suffered a heart attack. The doctors blamed his smoking, although he believed it to be more the result of stress. As he recovered from an angioplasty, he was visited by Gregory Evans. The pair were reconciled after five years of estrangement, and remain close to this day.

When he returned home, Hockney installed a treadmill in the studio – positioned in front of a television – and attempted a healthier diet, but otherwise threw himself back into his work. In spring 1991, he had to go to Chicago to finalise the lighting for *Turandot*. He decided to drive the 2,000 miles from Los Angeles in his Lexus, accompanied by Fitzherbert and their friends Richard Schmidt (his technical assistant on the stage designs) and Bing McGilvray, as well as Stanley and Boodgie. They took a second vehicle, a rented RV, to sleep and wash in, although they ended up staying mostly in motels.

The friends passed through the wildernesses of the American West and Rocky Mountains. On the long drive back to Los Angeles, on a beautiful Sunday afternoon, the RV broke down just past the continental divide in Colorado – the most spectacular setting, Hockney thought, that you could break down in, although a row soon erupted. Hockney was intent on filming everything, even the recovery of the RV. When Schmidt arranged for the vehicle to be towed early the next day, denying the opportunity to film, Hockney flew into a rage. 'He had a very bad temper,' Fitzherbert remembered. 'He loved that rage. It was almost like some kind of medicine for him.' Having kissed and made up, they detoured through Monument Valley, arriving just as the sun was setting. After spending the night in the RV, Hockney watched the dawn break over the valley.

Visions of the road trip filtered into his next series, *Very New Paintings* (*V.N. Paintings*). In these, the influence of his theatre designs coalesced with the American landscape in near-abstract compositions. The works were as close to non-figurative art as he had come since his college days, and yet their concern with space and volume linked them equally with his mountainous scenes of the previous year. He perceived, in this new series, the impact of the mountains and the sea, relentless forces of nature that were also quite sexual.

The *Very New Paintings* developed over a four-year period, interrupted frequently by Hockney's work on *Turandot* and *Die Frau ohne Schatten*. In 1992, some were made in Bridlington, the seaside Yorkshire town where his mother had now moved to live with his sister, Margaret, in a spacious 1920s house on the seafront, formerly a hotel. In November, Hockney was back in England for the premiere of *Die Frau ohne Schatten* at the Royal Opera House. The designs culminated with a grand assertion of the life force in the form of a human sperm – metamorphosed from a river – snaking across the final front cloth.

In the summer of 1994, Hockney went to Long Island to visit Henry Geldzahler, who was dying of pancreatic cancer. At Geldzahler's request, Hockney made a series of drawings of his sick friend. Recalling Don Bachardy's sketches of the dying Isherwood in 1986, these poignant valedictory portraits would feature in Hockney's drawing retrospective at the Hamburger Kunsthalle in 1995, travelling to the Royal Academy, London, and LACMA. One drawing shows Geldzahler asleep, propped up on a pillow, a frail vestige of his former self.

Geldzahler had been Hockney's great friend and confidant for thirty years; they had spoken on the phone virtually every day for twenty or thirty minutes. Footage from one of their summers on Fire Island shows Geldzahler lying with Hockney on a bed, cradling and caressing his friend – a vivid insight into their emotional bond. The curator had been one of the few people who didn't hesitate to tell Hockney what he liked and didn't like, or to criticise Hockney himself, albeit in the gentlest way. He once wrote an inventory of the artist's faults on a napkin. These included 'suffers fools gladly' and 'unintentionally rude'. In the years when Hockney's work, so invested in literature and music, had been at odds with the mainstream of contemporary art, Geldzahler's support had meant everything.

Reeling from his friend's death in August, Hockney retreated to Malibu and painted his dachshunds, Stanley and Boodgie, in multiple small oil sketches. He found that he had to paint rapidly, as the dogs didn't stay seated, or even asleep, in the same position for long. When he painted Stanley eating, he calculated that he had six minutes to make the picture. To avoid having to paint close to the floor, he constructed little platforms on which the dogs could rest. He began to sense that they somehow knew they were posing.

When two dozen of the dachshund paintings were shown at L.A. Louver in 1995, alongside *Very New Paintings* and drawings of friends, collectors were desperate to buy them. But Hockney refused to let go of them. In the summer, he sent fifty dog paintings to the 1853 Gallery in Saltaire, where Jonathan Silver was organising a Healing Festival in the aftermath of local riots.

That summer, Hockney was deeply affected by an exhibition of Claude Monet's paintings in Chicago. The experience of seeing Monet's work induced him to look with new wonder at such incidental details as a small shadow on Michigan Avenue, or light hitting a leaf. This, and a similarly inspiring display of Vermeer's work that he saw in The Hague, led to a new body of paintings of flowers and other still-life subjects. Some observers wondered what flowers had to do with Vermeer, but for Hockney it was the colour or 'glow' of the Dutch master that he was interested in replicating, more than his subject matter.

These works appeared, together with a sequence of oil paintings of friends, in an exhibition at Annely Juda Fine Art in London in May 1997. The gallery, run since 1968 by the German-born dealer Annely Juda and her son David, had begun representing Hockney in Britain after John Kasmin closed his Cork Street gallery – a fifteen-year partnership with New York's Knoedler gallery – in 1992. ('David Juda is the least slick dealer that I know, with a modest house,' Hockney has since remarked. 'He puts all his love into the gallery and always pays me promptly.') Entitled *Flowers, Faces and Spaces*, the show was his first at a London gallery for over a decade and attracted massive numbers of visitors – as well as an outpouring of negative press. In the view of Tom Lubbock in *The Independent*, Hockney's celebrity exceeded his current form: 'without the name, there wouldn't be such cause to write these pictures up … They prove nothing about what painting can do now, and they disprove nothing either.'

Hockney's personal life was shadowed by loneliness. His relationship with John Fitzherbert petered out in 1996 after an argument over some drawings Fitzherbert had sold, although the two remained close, emotionally and geographically: Fitzherbert moved (as Ian Falconer had done) into a house down the hill from Montcalm Avenue, paid for by Hockney. The artist's deafness continued to preclude large social gatherings. In August 1996, his old friend Ossie Clark was stabbed to death in his council flat by a former lover he had first picked up in Holland Park a year earlier. Clark had suffered a long, ignominious descent since his heyday in the mid-1970s. By the 1980s, he was bankrupt and sleeping on friends' sofas.

In the early summer of 1997, Hockney road-tripped through the American Southwest, visiting the Grand Canyon and re-experiencing its 'spatial thrill' and preternatural colour – what Vladimir Nabokov called 'the violet shade of pink cliffs'. That same summer, Jonathan Silver was diagnosed with terminal pancreatic cancer. After the death of Henry Geldzahler, Silver had become one of Hockney's closest friends; now he was succumbing to the same disease. In July, Hockney came to Yorkshire to be near his friend, a visit that would last for six months, the longest time he had spent in England for twenty years. While there, he converted the loft of the house in Bridlington where his sister and mother lived into a studio.

Silver had tried for many years to persuade Hockney to paint the Yorkshire landscape. Now, as the artist drove daily from the house in Bridlington to Wetherby on the other side of York, he finally embraced the idea. The surface of the land, he noticed, was changing all the time: when he arrived, farmers were just about to begin harvesting – the cornfields were golden. Big machines were getting ready in the fields, reminding him of pregnant insects laying eggs. His first three paintings of Yorkshire showed different parts of the sixty-mile journey: *North Yorkshire*, *The Road across the Wolds* and *The Road to York through Sledmere* (all 1997), the latter portraying a road dipping between glowing redbrick houses. *Salts Mill*, painted specially for Silver, depicts Silver's own lasting monument to Hockney, the 1853 Gallery.

'In a sense those Yorkshire paintings came out of the ideas of the great spaces of the West,' Hockney later remarked. Memories of his American road trip continued to reverberate. The works also carried echoes of his pictures of the Hollywood Hills with their meandering roads and vertiginous topography. He brought the unfinished canvases, still wet, to show to Silver, who told him: 'Paint those pictures, David. Keep on painting them. Life is a celebration, really.' *Salts Mill* was completed around ten days before Silver's death on 24 September 1997. His doctors said that his life had likely been prolonged by the delight of Hockney's visits and seeing the paintings develop.

# 9.
# The Great Wall: Yorkshire and Arizona, 1998–2001

Back in Los Angeles, Hockney continued to paint Yorkshire from memory – and its scenery continued to intersect, in his mind, with that of America. *Garrowby Hill* (1998), painted in three weeks, was the culmination of this first Yorkshire series. It evokes the view from the highest point of the Yorkshire Wolds, the road spilling downwards in the direction of a fifty-mile expanse of fields. Hockney had cycled up this hill as a teenager when he worked as a farmhand.

Following his tour through American wildernesses the previous summer, his thoughts were returning in particular to the Grand Canyon. In 1997, he had reprinted a large-scale version of a photo-collage of the canyon (photographed in 1982 and assembled in 1986) for a retrospective of his photographic work at the Ludwig Museum in Cologne, but was unhappy with the result, feeling that it was flat.

The painting *A Bigger Grand Canyon* (1998) was a fresh attempt to convey the sheer immensity of the setting. It consisted of sixty canvases arranged in a grid, and it evoked the spreading landmasses of the canyon in scorching reds and pinks, with the sky glimpsed at the upper edge as a thin band of blue. Painted between January and March, it was based closely on the sixty-part photo-collage. While he was working on the picture, he happened to meet fellow artist Ed Ruscha at a party. Leaving early, Hockney told Ruscha that he had to go home to bed in order to rise early, as he was making a large painting of the Grand Canyon. Ruscha replied: 'Well, in miniature, of course,' which Hockney found amusing – because any depiction of this subject, no matter its size, would be a miniature.

The second work, he resolved, shouldn't be based on photographs at all. He went to stay at the Grand Canyon for a week, sleeping in an old hotel only a few yards from Powell Point. He would take a chair to the cliff edge and sit gazing at the canyon, sometimes drawing, occasionally having thoughts that the whole thing might in fact be flat.

Hockney has called the canyon the world's biggest hole – a place without a centre or a focal point. He wanted to convey in painting the 'unphotographable' experience of standing at the boundary of this vast and complex space. When he returned to the studio, he painted *A Closer Grand Canyon* entirely from memory and drawings. Similar to the first version in its glowing colours, the work showed the view from the canyon's southern rim. It was the biggest picture he had made to date. The use of smaller canvases was a nod to the composite format of his photo-collages, as well as a matter of convenience: Hockney's largest paintings are easy to transport owing to their modular structure.

The Grand Canyon paintings were shown at the Centre Georges Pompidou in January 1999 as part of *Espace/ Paysage*, a career survey concentrating on themes of space and landscape. Simultaneously, Hockney staged an exhibition at the Musée Picasso in Paris, *Dialogue avec Picasso*, featuring a group of etchings made over the course of a year in Los Angeles, with the assistance of Maurice Payne.

Early 1999 was also the occasion of an exhibition at the National Gallery in London devoted to the work of Jean-Auguste-Dominique Ingres. This included small-scale drawings that Ingres had made of aristocratic Grand Tourists in Italy after the fall of the Napoleonic regime in 1815. When he went to see the show, Hockney was fascinated by the miniature scale and almost photographic precision of these drawings. He took the catalogue back to Los Angeles and studied the images and essays obsessively, wondering how Ingres had achieved such a flawless level of accuracy on such a small scale, drawing in smooth, uncorrected lines. The thought came to him that, rather like Warhol in his still-life drawings (which he had seen the year before at the New York gallery of Paul Kasmin, John's son), Ingres had traced the faces through some kind of projection technique. Ingres's lines seemed uncannily close to Warhol's – clean, fast, completely assured.

Hockney's intuition marked a turning point. Once he had noticed it with Ingres, he began to discern lens- or mirror-based imagery everywhere in the history of art. He would devote the next three years to an investigation of Western painting, exploring the hypothesis that the Old Masters used a simple form of camera to assist with the creation of their paintings. He stopped painting and became consumed by the research, which would culminate in a television documentary and a book in 2001, both titled *Secret Knowledge*.

As part of his investigation, he bought a *camera lucida*, an invention of the early nineteenth century consisting of a tiny prism on the end of a flexible metal rod. By looking through the lens, artists see their subject hovering over the surface of the paper beneath the device. Setting it up in a cosy, curtained-off alcove of his studio, Hockney used it to make a series of drawings of friends, relying on the lens to mark the spacing of the eyes and other basic features, before relying on his own observation or 'eyeballing'. In the course of making these works, Hockney became convinced that painters as far back as the Renaissance had used mirrors and lenses to create optical projections.

In early May of 1999, Laura Hockney's health rapidly declined. Hockney and his four siblings came to Bridlington to be with her. He drew her until close to the end, sitting up with her all night as she waited for the arrival of his brother John from Australia. She died, aged ninety-eight, three hours after John arrived. In the months following her death, Hockney stayed in London. Just as he had in the aftermath of Geldzahler's death, he concentrated on drawing his friends (creating, as the writer Lawrence Weschler has remarked, 'a sort of defiant inventory of the life that remains'), still using the *camera lucida*. Over the course of the following year, he made some 250 drawings, fifty-six of which were shown at Annely Juda that summer.

In late 1999, he developed his exploration of the *camera lucida* in a series of twelve drawings of wardens at the National Gallery, titled *12 Portraits after Ingres in a Uniform*

*Style*, for exhibition the following year. Each portrait in pencil, crayon and gouache shows a different guard from the gallery seated in their uniform (purple-blue shirts and jackets appended with gold badges). Each sitter presents the artist with the calm, inscrutable expression worn in their daily life. Often, the subject's hands appear enlarged due to the exaggerated perspective produced by the *camera lucida*.

The following year, Hockney pinned up a vast chronological sequence of photocopied images of paintings on the long wall of his studio at Montcalm Avenue, a giant collage that became known as *The Great Wall* – the middle ages marked one end, the nineteenth century the other, with northern Europe stretching along the top half, and southern Europe below. His conclusion was that Western art had suddenly embraced a photographic view of the world around the 1420s, and that this view had prevailed through to the late nineteenth century, the point at which 'awkwardness' returns to painting. Many art historians cast doubt on Hockney's theory, pointing out that there was little evidence that lenses had been used in such a way, or that they had existed before the 1600s. But there was early support from an experimental physicist and expert in optics, Charles M. Falco. Falco visited the studio and viewed *The Great Wall* – and made the fascinating suggestion that a concave mirror could have been deployed in the same way as a lens to project an image onto a canvas.

As a result, Hockney and Falco together developed a thesis that paintings such as Jan van Eyck's *Arnolfini Wedding* (1434) had been created by using a piece of concave glass, or a mirror, to create a traceable reflected image. Hockney had always been mystified by the complexity of the chandelier hanging above the couple in Van Eyck's picture, and the way its ornamented arms had been rendered with meticulous foreshortening. A clue to how it might have been accomplished lay, moreover, within the picture itself, in the convex mirror at the back of the scene. It was just the kind of mirror that would offer a suitable concave surface if it were turned around.

Hockney had a replica of the chandelier made and used a four-inch mirror to project it at the same size as in the painting. He then drew his own version of the chandelier to demonstrate how the projection ensured a faultless rendering. On a trip to Florence, he again used a mirror – positioned in the darkened doorway of the cathedral – to recreate the conditions under which Filippo Brunelleschi had painted the baptistry opposite the cathedral in perfect perspective, some twenty years before Van Eyck's painting. In a Hollywood studio, Hockney used models and props to restage tableaux by Vermeer, Caravaggio and other masters, which he then projected onto a darkened canvas by means of a mirror.

In December 2001, following the publication of Hockney's book *Secret Knowledge* and the broadcast of the television documentary chronicling his research, a conference was convened at the New York Institute for the Humanities. Artists, scientists and curators came together to debate – sometimes fractiously – the merits of his theory. Susan Sontag was among those who criticised it: 'it would be a bit like finding out that all the great lovers of history have been using Viagra'. Hockney himself maintained that the theory was precisely that – a hypothesis and not a conclusive statement.

The research leading to *Secret Knowledge* had been intense and exhausting (not to mention expensive), and Hockney was growing tired of the controversy that he had ignited among art historians and scientists. He was now determined to return to painting. During a spell in London, he had achieved another resurrection – of his relationship with John Fitzherbert. The pair resumed their old routine in Los Angeles, although their regained domesticity was interrupted when Hockney fell ill with pancreatitis, after which he was forced to give up alcohol and caffeine – a change that revivified his mood and energy.

In May 2001, Hockney's beloved dachshund Stanley had died, aged fifteen. Hockney and his housekeeper, Elsa, cried for two days. Stanley was buried in the garden at Montcalm Avenue. In November, Hockney's close friend Jeff Burkhart succumbed to AIDS. Burkhart, a larger-than-life Hollywood writer, had become a near-daily visitor to the house. These two losses helped to galvanise a decision to spend more time in London.

# 10.

# A Bigger Picture: Yorkshire, 2002–12

In the spring of 2002, Hockney sat for his old friend Lucian Freud. Each morning, he walked to Freud's Kensington house – dressed in the same chequered red jacket and blue shirt – and sat from 8.30 until noon. The portrait took 120 hours, spread over four months. Hockney was struck by the way Freud chatted while painting, in contrast to his own tendency to work in silence. He noticed, too, that Freud's paints were mostly similar colours, that he never replaced the caps on the tubes, and that it took him time to find the colour he wanted.

As Hockney sat, he and Freud – who called him 'The Yorkshire Master' – spoke about paintings and people, mostly gossiping about mutual acquaintances (Hockney admitted afterwards that he considered some of Freud's remarks cruel as well as funny). Hockney filled sketchbooks with drawings of the daily routine. Every morning, on his way to Freud's studio, he would walk through Holland Park. It was the first spring he had experienced in Britain for years, and he was arrested by how dramatic the change of season was by contrast with the uniform Mediterranean climate of California. In Freud's studio, he took the opportunity to sketch details of the dingy, paint-encrusted space – so different from his own studio – whenever Freud left to answer the phone.

Hockney had agreed to the portrait on condition that Freud would sit for him in return. But it was not an equal exchange. Freud's sitting, which took place in the summer, was confined to three hours – and Freud was unable to keep still. Hockney's pen-and-ink drawing conveys the older artist's awkwardness. Freud is shown sitting in a swivel chair, facing Hockney with an austere glare, while his frail body seems to shift uneasily. At one point in the process, Freud began to fall asleep.

That same year, Hockney returned to watercolours. He had never found the medium easy, owing to its techniques and tricks. Now he came to realise that the fully laden watercolour brush allowed a directness of mark-making, and a rapidity of flow, unlike anything else.

His subjects included still lifes and portraits of friends as they visited his studio in London. These evolved into a new sequence of double portraits in watercolour, in which pairs of friends appeared on the same office chairs positioned against a green wall. The first work in the group showed Sir George and Lady Christie, who had run Glyndebourne Opera – the setting of Hockney's first stage designs – for forty years. Painted from life in one day, the picture covered four large sheets of paper. Incongruously large for a watercolour, it shows the couple attired as if for a night at the opera, Mary in a shining white gown and pearl necklace, and George in black tie. Hockney's second two subjects were the daughters of his late friend Jonathan Silver, Davina and Zoe. As he drew them, he kept seeing the face of his friend. Davina observed a slightly mournful quality in the resulting picture.

Hockney regarded the watercolour portraits as stories. He created them rapidly, at a rate of four a week, relishing the challenge of having to think quickly as he worked from light to dark. At times, he found that he had to sacrifice accuracy or even a conventional likeness in favour of a sense of liveliness. He called the works *Portraits for the Twenty-First Century*, an ironic affirmation of the vitality of his medium. The relationships between the subjects varied: man and wife, brother and sister, two lovers. John Fitzherbert appeared twice, alongside each of his brothers. Hockney also persuaded Lucian Freud to sit for him again – this time alongside Freud's assistant, David Dawson. The watercolour was completed in three and a half hours, although Hockney knew that he was working with the benefit of having watched Freud for 120 hours during their earlier sittings. The curator Marco Livingstone, who sat with his partner Stephen Stuart-Smith, speculated that the artist was fascinated by all relationships – by any two people who can make a life together, given that he hadn't found this easy to achieve himself.

In the space of a few months, Hockney made some forty works. Engrossed in the project, he ended up staying in London far longer than he had intended: 2002 marked the longest period of time he had been away from California since 1978. Partly in order to find subjects for the series, he resumed his old London life, connecting with people he hadn't seen much of for thirty years.

In February 2003, Hockney and John Fitzherbert flew

back to Los Angeles. In early May, Fitzherbert returned to spend another week in London, and when he tried to re-enter the US, he was detained at the airport for having outstayed his visa on a previous visit – and then summarily deported. Strenuous attempts to secure his re-entry failed, and Hockney became lonely and resentful. And so he decamped to London again that summer, before going up to Yorkshire to be with his sister, whose partner, Ken, was dying. He stayed on after Ken's death in July and began to drive around the region with Margaret, rediscovering the landscape he had known as a child.

Hockney had never stopped returning to Yorkshire; for thirty years, he had spent Christmases at home with his mother. But he had always considered England too dark and too cold to stay for long. The summer of 2004 signalled the beginning of a prolonged return that would last for close to a decade. He moved into his sister's house in Bridlington together with John Fitzherbert and his new assistant, a Parisian accordionist called Jean-Pierre Gonçalves de Lima (JP), to whom he had been introduced by David Graves and his wife, Ann. Margaret moved out, to a house two streets away.

Before long, Hockney was enjoying his bohemian existence in Bridlington, undisturbed by his 'office' in Los Angeles until six o'clock in the evening. He would tell his Los Angeles friends that he was on location in Yorkshire. Aspects of British society still grated – the 'fucking Blairs', the nanny state, infringements of civil liberties (especially the 'mean-spirited' anti-smoking lobby); as well as a national treasure, he would come to be regarded as something of a 'moaner in chief'. But the English landscape had become a fascination. 'I wasn't going to stay here,' he subsequently admitted. 'But as things changed, and the corn got golden, I realised there's a fucking good subject here. So why should I go back to LA?'

Scouting the local area by car with JP ('the only Parisian in Bridlington'), Hockney began to capture the scenery in watercolour. The sketches were made on the spot from the low-slung passenger seat of his parked car – he carried his premixed watercolours in pill bottles. Thirty-six of these scenes were assembled into a work titled *Midsummer: East Yorkshire* (2004), a grid of intensely observed 'snapshots': a field of high corn, a village street, trees in full leaf and other deftly brushed vistas.

The watercolours were first exhibited at Salts Mill, followed by presentations at Somerset House, London, and (in February 2005) L.A. Louver. Contemplating the works on the wall of his studio, Hockney wryly compared them with the stacked monitors he had seen on television during the US election night coverage of 2 November 2004 – pointing out that whereas the streaming monitors (arrayed behind the anchor people) had been almost illegible, his views of Yorkshire delivered a wealth of 'focused scrutiny' across the wall. On a return trip to LA in spring 2005, Hockney began to use oil paint once more, while working on a group of portraits of friends. Back in Bridlington in the summer, he returned to many of the scenes he had sketched the previous year – this time using oil rather than watercolour. He continued to work *en plein air* in the manner of the Impressionists and Constable. He and JP started out at dawn each day. Driving around the Yorkshire Wolds, they saw little other traffic apart from agricultural vehicles. Once they had found a suitable view, they would set up an easel and table. Hockney worked on two-by-three-foot canvases, completing them at a rate of around one a day, usually in perfect solitude, although occasionally a farmer would come by to chat and observe.

One of the spots he settled on was a farm track that he came to refer to as the 'Tunnel', as the trees formed a dark avenue, their overhanging foliage creating a spiral of light and shade. Hockney soon decided that he wanted to work on a much larger scale. He brought six canvases to the spot, producing a large composite scene entitled *A Closer Winter Tunnel, February–March 2006*, in which the track recedes – scored by two red-brown furrows – between leafless trees. While painting the scene, he moved between the six canvases, assembling them periodically into a grid to assess the overall composition. At the start of each day, before driving to the setting, he would review a digital collage of the work. He painted the Tunnel seven times in the course of a year, over the changing seasons. Another subject that he returned to repeatedly was a dead tree that he called the Totem – a lopped trunk, isolated like a pillar.

Hockney invested in a four-wheel-drive Toyota pickup truck, in which multiple wet canvases could be stacked, and drove out every day to the sites he was painting. A clearing in Woldgate Woods became another favourite setting. Immersed in his new project, he spent his first full winter in Britain for some thirty years. In early 2006, he was further inspired by a Constable retrospective at

Tate Britain, where he took note of the ambitious scale of Constable's oil sketches.

By this time, Hockney had gathered around him a small circle of friends and assistants, similar to the team who continued to manage his home at Montcalm Avenue, LA. Living together in the seafront house, they enjoyed an intimate and permissive existence, although Hockney himself was more restrained with drugs and alcohol than in earlier years: 'I don't go out that much. Frankly, my life's mostly reading and painting, and a few nights of nice sex.' The tweed-suited figure of the artist became a common sight on the promenade, as he walked to buy cigarettes in the early morning or treated his team of young assistants to breakfast at the local café. An interviewer visiting in 2009 observed a freeform ambience in which Fitzherbert ('friendly, quietly efficient and prone to fits of giggles') presided on the domestic front, while other characters came in and out: Hockney's new technical assistant Jonathan Wilkinson, for instance, and various '[s]hy local boys, helpers about the house or studio'.

In the summer of 2006, Hockney flew to Los Angeles for the opening of a retrospective of his portraits at LACMA, which was travelling from the Museum of Fine Arts, Boston, and would subsequently move to the National Portrait Gallery, London. The event was an unwelcome interruption from his labours in Yorkshire, and he was frustrated to be missing the hawthorn blossom. But by assembling reproductions of his Yorkshire pictures on the wall at home in LA, he had the opportunity to review the previous year's output. This gave him the idea of working on a yet grander scale.

At the start of his third year in Yorkshire, Hockney asked the Royal Academy for the use of the end wall of its largest gallery during that year's Summer Exhibition – and was granted permission. He then set about making a painting to fit. The subject was a crop of tall trees close to the village of Warter, dominated by a vast sycamore. He depicted the scene from close up, section by section, working on a group of canvases at a time, and alternating between the physical site and his Bridlington studio. He was able to view a fifth of the overall painting, which would ultimately consist of fifty canvases, at any one time. Only through digital photography was he able to map out the work's total appearance, inserting a photograph of each section into a computerised jigsaw of the whole. Otherwise, the image existed solely in his head and in drawings. He spent hours at the location near Warter, sometimes more or less lying down to study the intertwining branches.

Hockney completed the painting, his largest ever, in a two-week period in March 2007, just before the trees broke into leaf. *Bigger Trees near Warter or/ou Peinture sur le motif pour le Nouvel Age Post-Photographique* measures fifteen by forty feet, and shows the trees rising and splitting into a vast system of overcrossing branches, silhouetted against a bone-white sky, with two small redbrick houses squatting at the bottom right of the panorama. Before the work was shipped to the Royal Academy, Hockney hired an industrial unit and had carpenters construct a vast plywood wall on which the painting could be assembled. When a delegation of curators and critics from London came to view the work, they found Hockney and JP dramatically changed: both had grown beards during their weeks of labour. While JP seemed exhausted, Hockney was sparkling with energy.

While making his gargantuan landscape, Hockney had designed a tongue-in-cheek poster, announcing the work's display at the Royal Academy:

COMING UP AT THE ROYAL ACADEMY
A BIGGER SENSATION
A HANDMADE OIL PAINTING
Recently done *en plein air* by D. Hockney RA

The wording was an allusion to the Royal Academy's *Sensation* exhibition of 1997, which had brought the conceptualist work of the Young British Artists of the 1990s to wide public attention. Fifteen years on, Hockney believed he was staging a similarly groundbreaking event (if not more so: a bigger sensation). His painting, he claimed, was an affirmation of the post-photographic age.

As the piece was installed on the end wall of Gallery III, Hockney directed proceedings from a borrowed electric wheelchair. Perhaps inevitably, the scale and prominence of the work prompted muttering among the other academicians. But the upshot was that the Royal Academy's curator of contemporary art, Edith Devaney, asked him if he would stage a solo exhibition focusing on his Yorkshire landscapes. He agreed, on condition that it could be in 2012, as he would need four more springs. Inspired by Picasso's remark, 'Give me a museum and I'll fill it,' he began to conceive a display filling the entire Academy.

While looking for storage space, Hockney had come across a warehouse three minutes away from his house in Bridlington. It was on the same industrial estate as the unit where he had installed *Bigger Trees near Warter*, but far larger. Attracted by the even light flooding through the ceiling, he decided to transform it into a gigantic new studio. Upon signing the lease, he said he felt twenty years younger. The Atelier, as he came to call it, would be the setting of the most prolific phase of his career – and was large enough to incorporate a full-scale replica of the Royal Academy galleries. In addition to his paintings *en plein air*, he now made works from memory, based on long periods of looking at a given site: for instance, the vast picture *Winter Timber* (2009), in which orange-yellow felled logs streak in clusters along a purple track. A large composite photograph from 2011 captures the leisurely 'salon' atmosphere of the Atelier: friends young and old, including Fitzherbert, sit and stand around – smoking, resting on the sofa, treating the dogs or working at a large studio table. Hockney's romantic bond with Fitzherbert had waned again, and yet – like other former lovers – Fitzherbert remained a core member of the household.

Hockney's international kudos received a fresh boost in May 2009, when his painting *Beverly Hills Housewife* (1966) sold for $7.9 million at Christie's, New York, in the depths of a recession – breaking a previous record of $5.35 million for *The Splash* in 2006. Betty Freeman, the subject of the portrait, had died that January. Hockney would admit a few years later that the auction prices left him amazed, although as to whether he was overvalued, he demurred: 'When I look at some other things I think, well, maybe I am. But when I look at some other things I think, well, maybe I am not.'

A more personal milestone was Hockney's visit to the Frick Collection in New York in 2010. He was struck – not for the first time – by Claude Lorrain's *The Sermon on the Mount* (1656). The painting, with its scene of a steep outcrop of land rising in front of the sea, became a totem. Hockney progressively 'cleaned' the image in Photoshop to recover the original hues (long since obscured as a result of a fire in the eighteenth century) and scrutinised it intently, often as he lay in bed. The picture became the object of a series of variations and studies, culminating in the grand-scaled painting *A Bigger Message* (2010), his own secular Sermon on the Mount.

Margaret Hockney had been an early convert to the iPhone and in 2009 told her brother about a new drawing app, Brushes. On his own phone, he began to make drawings with this 'free medium' using his thumb: usually sunrises and flowers (John Fitzherbert began to buy a bouquet of flowers every day), as well as still-life details such as a pair of slippers. Early on, Hockney would rub his thumb on his clothes – by instinct – before changing to a different colour. He especially liked to draw the dawn through the window of his bedroom as he lay in bed. Friends would receive a new drawing every morning, and soon he had to buy a second iPhone because he had filled up the memory on the first.

The following April, Hockney bought an iPad imme-diately upon its release by Apple. Now using his finger to draw, he mastered the variety of techniques available, including the use of a stylus to achieve finer marks. He was thrilled by the speed of the medium and declared that Picasso would have gone mad for it. The drawings he created, many of them outdoors, were similar to those he made on the iPhone, but with the added advantage that he was able to replay the formation of the work, mark by mark. For the first time, he felt that he was able to watch himself draw. The iPad became an indispensable item in the large 'poacher's pocket' of his jacket.

The previous spring, Hockney had made a film from a moving car of the hawthorn blossom. This shaky handheld footage was the beginning of an ambitious project of filming the landscape from a moving vehicle. Nine cameras were rigged on a slow-moving jeep, with Hockney observing the nine simultaneous recordings on nine monitors in the back. The result was a new cinematic variant on the 'joiner' format of the 1980s: a grid of misaligned recordings captured at a dream-like pace. When he presented the works for the first time, to a group of friends in his Santa Monica studio, Hockney joined two sets of nine screens together to make an eighteen-part composite.

January 2012 marked the opening of *David Hockney: A Bigger Picture* at the Royal Academy in London, an exhibition five years in the planning. Dominated by his paintings of Yorkshire, the presentation was a tour de force of scale and ambition. Marco Livingstone, the show's curator, observed that in eight years Hockney – seized by manic productivity – had made a lifetime's work. The largest work on display, *The Arrival of Spring in Woldgate, East Yorkshire in 2011 (twenty eleven)*, was a gallery-sized installation of fifty-one iPad prints around three walls – an orchestral chronicling of the shift, day by day, from winter to summer – together with a massive painting occupying the final wall. Formed from thirty-two canvases, the painting depicts a path leading through a clearing towards a cluster of trees; their bright green leaves float on the ends of serpentine stems, above a forest floor teeming with ferns.

Critical responses were as variegated as the works themselves, although largely admiring. In *The Times*, Rachel Campbell-Johnston wrote that '*A Bigger Picture* feels like one of those exhibitions that form a rare landmark in our cultural history … These works are not the retreat of a celebrated painter into mellow nostalgia. They trumpet perceptions that remain as passionate as those of youth.' Predictable vitriol issued from Brian Sewell in *The Evening Standard*: 'I must ask, if he is not purblind, from whom he borrows this jangling, jarring, grating palette? In this new work, every blade of grass, every stalk of stubble, every hedgerow flower is reduced to a cypher and, when diminished by erratic perspective, to a blur.' Many critics were in tune with the qualified admiration of Laura Cumming in *The Observer*: '*A Bigger Picture* is radiantly bright, spectacularly large in both scale and extent and ebullient to the point of jubilation' – an effusion to which she added the thudding counterweight: 'the results are bafflingly low on singularity, emotion or depth.' Critical debate aside, the exhibition was spectacularly popular: over half a million people went to see it.

In late 2012, Hockney suffered a minor stroke. Gregory Evans, who was with him in London at the time, noticed that he couldn't finish sentences or answer questions. Evans also perceived a change in his drawings: there was suddenly more definition in them. Hockney underwent an operation to ease the effects. While he was in hospital, the Totem – the lopped tree trunk he had fallen in love with in Yorkshire and painted many times – was chopped down after being coated in graffiti. Hockney was plunged into a two-day depression. When he emerged from bed, he made four charcoal drawings of the Totem lying in the snow. Still unable to speak much, he reasoned that at least he could draw – a form of speaking.

Twenty-two years after he had turned down a knighthood, Hockney was awarded the Order of Merit in the New Year's Honours, joining the highly select group of artists, scientists and public servants to have received the accolade: Lucian Freud, who had died the previous year, had previously been the only painter in the order, which never numbers more than twenty-four living individuals. Hockney's acceptance of the honour was accompanied by another refusal, however. He felt compelled to turn down an invitation to paint the Queen owing to his work commitments, as well as a feeling that 'majesty' couldn't easily be rendered in a contemporary painting.

# 11.

# La Grande Cour: California, Normandy, 2013–Now

On 17 March 2013, Hockney's assistant Dominic Elliott died. Elliott, who was twenty-three, had been drinking and taking drugs with John Fitzherbert at the house in Bridlington while Hockney slept upstairs. Their late-night session – not an unusual occurrence in itself – took a tragic turn when Elliott drank from a bottle of domestic acid. Fitzherbert drove him to hospital in Scarborough but he was pronounced dead.

Elliott had been a key member of Hockney's tight-knit Bridlington team. He can occasionally be glimpsed in the documentary films shot during the artist's Yorkshire years. In a charcoal drawing made two months before his death, he appears contemplative, gazing into space with his fingers interlocking across the front of his thick jumper. He and Fitzherbert had been in a relationship, following the end of the latter's partnership with Hockney. But the reasons for Elliott's self-destructive act – beyond the mind-altering effects of a bender – are unknown. The tragedy attracted widespread media attention. Hockney was devastated and unable to work. His project of landscape drawings in charcoal – a sequence of scenes he had previously painted in watercolour or oil, each observed in five stages as spring developed – was temporarily abandoned.

After nine years, Hockney returned to Los Angeles in the summer of 2013, ahead of his solo exhibition at the de Young Museum, San Francisco, that October. He and some of his friends maintained that it was the show that had induced him to move, but he was haunted by what had happened in Yorkshire. Back in the Hollywood Hills, he tentatively began to draw in the garden. In July, he was getting ready to make a painting of the garden when he decided – on an impulse – to paint his assistant, JP, instead. Hockney had noticed him sitting with his head in his hands, in a pose similar to that of the sorrowful old man in Van Gogh's painting *At Eternity's Gate* (1890). Hockney regarded the image as a kind of self-portrait, bearing witness to the sorrow and impasse of the moment.

This image of despondency was the unlikely point of genesis of a new series of portraits in acrylic – the medium he had embraced when he first came to Los Angeles half a century earlier. Made on identically sized canvases, these show different sitters in the same yellow upholstered chair. The next two portraits were of his assistants Bing McGilvray, who remarked that Hockney had painted him looking like a refrigerator salesman, and Gregory Evans. He re-angled the chair a little between each portrait, and periodically swapped around the blue and green of the 'floor' and 'wall' that formed the pictures' two-tone backdrops (a formula that he had employed in oil portraits a decade earlier). By seating his subjects on a raised platform, he was able to obtain a good view of their feet.

The series spiralled over the following three years, propelled by the new energy and optimism Hockney was feeling since his return to Los Angeles. Subjects included his family, friends and the children of friends. His eighty-seven-year-old dentist ('a very funny man, unusually for a dentist') was captured six weeks before his death. Working in silence, Hockney would paint for six to seven hours a day, and usually spent three days on a given painting – he referred to the pictures as 'twenty-hour exposures'. In each case he began by sketching his subject in charcoal straight onto the canvas, taking only forty-five minutes for this preliminary stage. The writer and critic Martin Gayford observed how, 'Occasionally, in a tone a little like that of a surgeon saying, "scalpel please", he asked J-P to squeeze some paint from a tube on to his palette. "Can you give me some cadmium yellow?"; "A neutral grey, please".'

The art dealer Larry Gagosian and certain other time-strapped sitters (including the artist John Baldessari and the architect Frank Gehry) only gave him two days. Gagosian reflected afterwards that he hadn't held his stomach in enough during the sessions. In an interview, Hockney quipped that Gagosian was always trying to persuade him to show with him – but that he wouldn't agree because Larry would want to sell everything. Also included in the series were Peter Goulds, the founder of L.A. Louver, and Douglas Baxter from Pace gallery, the artist's New York representative since 2008. 'I was very jet-lagged. I kept nodding off,' Baxter confessed. 'And at the end, David said, "I didn't really get you."'

Fourteen of the new portraits featured in *A Bigger Exhibition*, a 300-work survey of his output since 2002, which opened at the de Young Museum in October 2014. This also included the now-completed group of twenty-five charcoal landscapes, *The Arrival of Spring in 2013*, together with sombre charcoal portraits from the same period. Gregory Evans, who curated the show, was quoted in the catalogue as saying that he perceived a strong sense of mortality in the portraits. Reviewing the exhibition in *The New York Times*, Roberta Smith wrote:

> David Hockney is in one of his primes … As many people in the art world did, I resisted [his work] for years, finding it ingratiating and illustrative, more drawing than painting and (O.K., snobbishly) seeing its very popularity as a sign of weakness. But after a while his art was just doing too many interesting things to be resisted.

The final work in the long sequence of portraits, painted in November 2015, was an image of solemn, curious youth. The sitter was the eleven-year-old son of British artist Tacita Dean, Rufus. Dean had recently made a short film about Hockney, in which he appears surrounded by his own portraits, laughing, smoking and looking. When she brought her son along to the studio, Hockney was delighted by his eager questions, and so asked Dean if he could paint the boy's portrait. Rufus, who appears in a waistcoat and red tie, facing the artist head-on, pointed out afterwards that Hockney had given him blue eyes, whereas their real colour was brown, but that otherwise the likeness was perfect.

Life at Montcalm Avenue was, by this time, calmer than in earlier days – no longer the 'Mont Hysterical' that Henry Geldzahler had known. For years, Hockney's deafness had entailed a phased retreat from the social world: he only went to dinners 'under protest', and music was now lost to him. He was happiest when working. LA suited his desire for privacy and seclusion: 'You get in your car and go to someone else's house, and you're not meeting people on the street like in London or New York. It's great for that.' Even so, he noted with curiosity that a new art scene was developing around him in LA – due in part to the unaffordability of New York. His former assistant Charlie Scheips quipped that the world now came to David. The artist's LA team carried on busily around him – a nine-strong band of friends, assistants and former lovers, spread between the house and the archive on Santa Monica Boulevard. At its core were JP and Gregory Evans, the latter now in his early sixties.

In the evenings, Hockney was typically in bed by nine, having unplugged his hearing aids. His militancy of spirit hadn't deserted him, however. The vigorous work ethic of his earliest days as an artist, traipsing around Bradford with a pram of materials, remained strong. And he was still smoking prolifically, enjoying Camel Wides cigarettes; he liked to boast he had lived longer than his virulently anti-smoking father. In the judgment of Simon Hattenstone, writing in *The Guardian* in 2015, 'Hockney is such a militant smoker you sense he sparks up even when he doesn't fancy one, just to piss people off.' A shop in Hollywood provided him with a steady supply of cannabis: he carried a Medical Marijuana Patient Verification card stating that the drug was for anxiety – a handy pretext.

For his exhibition *82 Portraits and 1 Still-life*, which opened at the Royal Academy in London in July 2016,

Hockney presented the portrait series as a single work of art. The one still-life picture in the series was rendered in the same brilliant palette as the portraits: an assortment of fruit (lemons, apples, bananas) on a painted wooden bench. It was painted by chance, when one of Hockney's models missed a sitting and he didn't want to waste the paint.

The same year also saw the publication of a gigantic illustrated book, published by Benedikt Taschen (a near neighbour in Los Angeles), of his sixty-year corpus, featuring 450 works of art. Titled *A Bigger Book*, this 'sumo'-scale volume, as the publisher billed it, weighed almost 70lb and came with its own tripod stand. Not generally inclined to look back at the earlier phases of his career, Hockney admitted to feeling gratified as he surveyed the sum total of his output. He reflected, in particular, that the years from 1960 to 2000 – from his college days to the end of the twentieth century – had been among the freest there have ever been. From his time at the RCA onwards, he has lived in bohemia – a place of radical tolerance – whether in London or Los Angeles, Paris or Bridlington, although in recent years he has lamented the disappearance of this permissive state of being: 'Bohemia was against the suburbs, and now the suburbs have taken over. ... I mean, the anti-smoking thing is all anti-bohemia.'

In his Los Angeles studio, Hockney had meanwhile embarked on a group of multifigure paintings and photographs, a marked departure from the preceding series of single-subject portraits. These included scenes of people seated and wandering in the studio, card-players inspired by Cézanne, and a subseries of 'photographic paintings', in which he assembled hundreds of digital photographs (images of heads, shoes, jackets, tables and walls) into complex composites. Echoing the mosaic construction of his 1980s photo-collages, these extended and amplified his long-term experiments with multiple perspectives, and in particular the unconventionality of reverse perspective, whereby objects swell in proportion as they recede into the picture. Hockney called the effect of the collages '3-D without the glasses'.

At the same time, Hockney was preparing to review his legacy more comprehensively in the shape of a major retrospective at Tate Britain in 2017, touring to the Centre Georges Pompidou and the Metropolitan Museum of Art. Opening five months before his eightieth birthday, the Tate show was the most popular ever staged at the museum. The market value of his work, already hefty, was sent soaring by this latest testament to his career. In November 2017, *Portrait of an Artist (Pool with Two Figures)* (1972) – which appeared on the cover of the Tate catalogue – would be auctioned at Christie's for $90.3 million, setting a world auction record for a painting by a living artist. (Hockney remained as insouciant as ever about his work's market value: 'It is just a madness to me but I can't do anything about it so I just ignore it.')

Also in 2017, Hockney hit upon a new format. He began to paint on hexagonal canvases – similar to conventional oblong canvases, but with the bottom corners shaved off. The first painting was a scene of two vases of flowers on separate tables. The composition reminded him of Fra Angelico's *Annunciation* (1440–45), so next he painted his own version of the scene, translating the arching portico of the fifteenth-century fresco into an outspreading origami-like structure. The final painting of the show at the Metropolitan Museum was a depiction of his garden at Montcalm Avenue, the blue-painted decking wrapped around the bottom edge of the picture, with the pool and massed vegetation beyond. The indented bottom corners ironically enhanced the illusion of space in the picture's foreground, inviting fresh lines of sight.

The amended shape was a revelation. Hockney freely admitted that he couldn't understand why he hadn't chopped off the corners of his paintings twenty years earlier. Pursuing this line of thought, he returned – in several of the other hexagonal pictures – to earlier subjects including Garrowby Hill and the Hotel Acatlán in Mexico.

In another return to an earlier motif, Hockney decided to mark his eightieth birthday in July by repainting the sides of his pool in Los Angeles, which he had first adorned in 1982. The assigned date for creating the new version – a swarm of blue arabesques similar to the original – was 9 July, the day before his birthday. Despite it being the hottest day of the year so far, he started early in the morning and finished the work in under three hours.

The previous year, Hockney had received a commission that seemed to seal his status at the heart of the British establishment. The Dean of Westminster Abbey, the Very Reverend Dr John Hall, wanted to install a permanent commemoration to Elizabeth II, marking the sixty-fifth year of her reign. And so he approached Hockney – as Britain's 'most celebrated living artist', and moreover a figure whose career had run in parallel to the Queen's reign – to design a new stained-glass window for the Abbey's north transept, in a space previously filled with blank nineteenth-century glass.

Within a day of being offered the job, Hockney had sent the Dean a draft design. He had never worked in coloured glass, although the backlit screen of the iPad made it a perfect tool for the design. Based on the Yorkshire countryside, his vibrantly shaded scheme was also inspired by the other-worldly colours of Matisse and Chagall (both of whom had worked in stained glass). His drawing was translated into glass at a specialist studio in York, out of glass that had been handmade in Bavaria. The single fragment that Hockney painted himself was the pane bearing his signature – this had to be flown to Los Angeles for him to inscribe.

Spread across the Gothic tracery of the tall, pointed window, the nine-metre-high scene consisted of a country-side path – a brilliant red throughway – snaking between trees and a hawthorn bush whose exploding blossom gave the impression, Hockney thought, of champagne having been poured across the foliage. He felt that his own work compared favourably with the nineteenth-century design in the adjacent window, a representation of the miracles of Christ that was so dark as to be almost illegible. In October 2018, the Queen's Window was unveiled and dedicated in a special service, with Hockney present. The Dean remarked that although the monarch had been shown a sketch of the design, it was difficult to gauge her reactions to such things.

Dreading the long flight back to Los Angeles, Hockney decided to delay his return. JP suggested a three-day break in northern France. And so they set out for Normandy, where they visited the Bayeux Tapestry, which Hockney hadn't seen physically since the 1960s. He was enthralled, once more, by its graphic power (he noted the complete absence of shadows or reflections) and its narrative sequence, qualities that reminded him of Chinese scrolls. They also saw the fourteenth-century Apocalypse Tapestry in Angers. In the evening, as they watched the sun set over the docks at Le Havre, Hockney reflected that he would like to witness the arrival of spring in France, where there is more blossom than in east Yorkshire, even though, as he once observed, Normandy is topographically similar to the Yorkshire Wolds: a system of chalk hills divided by tiny dry valleys.

This was the beginning of the latest – ongoing – phase in Hockney's life. On their way to Paris to see a third masterpiece of European tapestry – *The Lady and the Unicorn* at the Musée de Cluny – he and JP stopped off to view a seventeenth-century farmhouse called La Grande Cour, set in four acres of orchards at the end of a gravel drive, and surrounded by level fields. Hockney fell in love with the 'seven dwarfs' house with its irregular elm beams and steeply gabled roof. After twenty-five minutes, he had decided to buy it. Builders were hired to create a new high-tech studio in an old cider press adjacent to the farmhouse. By March 2019, Hockney had moved in.

He spent the spring drawing and painting the Normandy house and its surroundings. He was now in his early eighties, but his enthusiasm for work was undiminished. His subjects were all around him, in contrast to Yorkshire, where he had had to drive out to his motifs. One painting, showing the pond alongside the house, was titled *Some Smaller Splashes* (2019) – an ironic nod to the Californian pool paintings of the 1960s. The scene of rain falling on water reminded him, too, of watching the sea billowing around his house in Malibu as he sat drinking tea with Celia Birtwell. In a twenty-four-part suite of drawings, *La Grande Cour*, he created a 360° panorama of his new property inspired by the Bayeux Tapestry. In the summer, he expanded his focus to include the nearby village of Beuvron-en-Auge, while also capturing the apple and pear trees in his garden.

Hockney was in the midst of depicting the winter trees when the coronavirus pandemic erupted. During the phases of lockdown that followed, he remained in his Normandy home with JP and his other long-term assistant, Jonathan Wilkinson, along with his dog Ruby. He wasn't bothered by the enforced isolation – it guaranteed an unbroken period of work. More than ever, Hockney's international celebrity was at odds with his secluded existence, supported and protected by a loyal inner circle (smaller now than the entourages of previous years). He kept in touch with intimate friends, such as Birtwell, on FaceTime – sometimes the pair would be in a dressing gown and hair curlers respectively as they chatted. Otherwise, he turned his energy and concentration towards the arrival of spring, just as he had a decade earlier in Yorkshire. Rising as early as five o'clock, he drew on his iPad in the open air, capturing the gradual metamorphosis of bare trees into leaves, and revelling in the variety of blossoms. Evenings were spent relaxing with cigarettes and non-alcoholic beer – and, in the absence of a television, books. 'The only real things in life are food and love in that order, just like our little dog Ruby,' he confessed in an interview. 'I really believe this and the source of art is love.'

At the height of the first wave of the pandemic, Hockney released an image of daffodils, drawn on his iPad, which he titled *Do Remember They Can't Cancel the Spring*. He then published ten images and an animation via the BBC, accompanied by a short article in which he professed: 'I love life.' He resolved to make a substantial group of iPad paintings, many of them to be printed and shown at the Royal Academy in 2021.

The lockdowns of 2020 marked an extended phase of isolation and work that has been one of the most productive in his life. He reread George Eliot's novel *Middlemarch* and Gustave Flaubert's *Sentimental Education*, the latter all about Normandy. Hockney's proliferation of scenes of Normandy – his house, grounds and other visions of daily life – were accumulating all the while into their own version of a realist French novel.

On 21 December 2020, the cover of *The New Yorker* showed Hockney's fireplace at La Grande Cour – an iPad-rendered image of flames shooting from an ironwork grate. It was a timely symbol of hope and a testament to the artist's undimmed energy as he advanced plans for an epic cycle of ten-metre-wide canvases in 2021, documenting the seasons over the course of the year. In a short video recorded around this time, he equated this energy with a capacity to see the world with absolute clarity: 'The world is very, very beautiful if you look at it. But most people don't look very much. They scan the ground in front of them so they can walk, but they don't really look at things incredibly well, with an intensity. I do, and I've always known that.'

# Bibliography


**Selected Books and Catalogues**

Peter Adam, *David Hockney and his Friends* (Bath: Absolute Press, 1997).

Richard Benefield et al, *David Hockney: A Bigger Picture*, exh. cat. (San Francisco: Fine Arts Museums of San Francisco; New York: DelMonico Books, 2013).

Martin Friedman (ed.), *Hockney Paints the Stage*, exh. cat. (Minneapolis: Walker Art Center; New York: Abbeville; London: Thames & Hudson, 1983).

Martin Gayford, *A Bigger Message: Conversations with David Hockney* (London: Thames & Hudson, 2011).

Mark Glazebrook (ed.), *David Hockney: Paintings, Prints, Drawings*, exh. cat. (London: Whitechapel Art Gallery, 1970).

David Hockney, *David Hockney by David Hockney: My Early Years*, ed. Nikos Stangos (London: Thames & Hudson, 1976).

——, 'Vogue par David Hockney', *Vogue*, no. 662, Paris, December 1985–January 1986, cover, pp. 219–59.

——, *That's the Way I See It*, ed. Nikos Stangos (London: Thames & Hudson, 1993).

——, *Secret Knowledge: Rediscovering the Lost Techniques of the Old Masters* (London: Thames & Hudson, 2001).

——, Hans Werner Holzwarth, *David Hockney: A Bigger Book* (Cologne: Taschen, 2016).

Marco Livingstone, *David Hockney* (London: Thames & Hudson, 2017, revised edition).

——, Edith Devaney et al, *David Hockney: A Bigger Picture*, exh. cat. (London: Royal Academy of Arts, 2012).

Paul Melia (ed.), *David Hockney* (Manchester; New York: Manchester University Press, 1995).

Alain Sayag, David Hockney, *David Hockney: Photographs*, exh. cat. (London; New York: Petersburg Press, 1982).

Stephen Spender, Pierre Restany, *David Hockney: Tableaux et Dessins/Paintings & Drawings*, exh. cat. (Paris: Musée des Arts Décoratifs, 1974).

Chris Stephens, Andrew Wilson (eds), *David Hockney*, exh. cat. (London: Tate Publishing, 2017).

Christopher Simon Sykes, *Hockney: The Biography, Volume I, 1937–1975 – A Rake's Progress* (London: Century, 2011).

——, *Hockney: The Biography, Volume II, 1975–2012 – A Pilgrim's Progress* (London: Century, 2014).

Maurice Tuchman (ed.), *David Hockney: A Retrospective*, exh. cat. (Los Angeles: Los Angeles County Museum of Art, 1988).

Peter Webb, *Portrait of David Hockney* (London: Chatto & Windus, 1988).

Lawrence Weschler, *True to Life: Twenty-Five Years of Conversations with David Hockney* (Berkeley; Los Angeles; London: University of California Press, 2008).

## Selected Film and TV

*Portrait of David Hockney*, directed by David Pearce, 1972.

*A Bigger Splash*, directed by Jack Hazan, 1974.

*A Day on the Grand Canal with the Emperor of China (or Surface Is Illusion But So Is Depth)*, directed by Philip Haas, written and narrated by David Hockney, 1988.

*David Hockney: Pleasures of the Eye*, directed by Gero von Boehm, 1996.

*David Hockney: In Perspective*, directed by Monique Lajournade, 1999.

*David Hockney: Double Portrait*, directed by Christopher Swayne and Bruno Wollheim, 2003.

*David Hockney: A Bigger Picture*, directed by Bruno Wollheim, 2009.

*Hockney*, directed by Randall Wright, 2014.

# Index

Artworks are noted in *italic*

# Acknowledgements

I am grateful to Randall Wright for his guidance and insights, as well as for the revelations contained in his film of 2014, *Hockney*. This short biography is indebted to the longer accounts of Peter Webb and Christopher Simon Sykes, as well as Hockney's own autobiographical volumes, edited by Nikos Stangos. I have drawn at various moments upon the conversations published by Lawrence Weschler and Martin Gayford, each of whom has become a kind of amanuensis to the artist. Art-historical scholarship – notably that of Marco Livingstone – has also been a vital touchstone. Numerous other sources have been invaluable in building a picture of Hockney's art and life: a selection appears in the bibliography. I would like to extend special thanks to Robert Shore and Marc Valli from Laurence King Publishing.

# Picture Credits

(numbered in order of appearance)

1. Photo © Geoffrey Reeve/Bridgeman Images
2. © Hulton-Deutsch Collection/Corbis via Getty Images
3. Photo 12/Alamy
4. Photo by Moviestore/Shutterstock
5. © Hulton-Deutsch Collection/Corbis via Getty Images
6. Robert Doisneau/Gamma-Rapho/Getty Images
7. Chris Morphet/Redferns/Getty Images
8. Michael Childers/Corbis via Getty Images
9 + 10. Frédéric Reglain/Gamma-Rapho via Getty Images
11. Photo by Keith Dobney/The Independent/Shutterstock
12. Bridgeman Images
13. © Basil Langton/Mary Evans Picture Library
14. Yann Gamblin/Paris Match via Getty Images
15. Photo by Lynn Hilton/ANL/Shutterstock
16. Peter Macdiarmid/Getty Images
17. Robin Utrecht/EPA/EFE/Shutterstock